Home Care:
An Alternative to the Nursing Home

Home Care:
An Alternative to the Nursing Home

Florine Du Fresne

The Brethren Press, Elgin, Ill.

HOME CARE
An Alternative to the Nursing Home

Copyright © 1983, by The Brethren Press, Elgin, Ill.

Cover photo by Vista III Design, Minneapolis, Minn.

Library of Congress Cataloging in Publication Data

Du Fresne, Florine.
    Home care : an alternative to the nursing home.

        1. Home nursing.   I. Title.   [DNLM: 1. Home nursing.
    2. Home care services.   3. Terminal care.   WY 200
    D864a]
    RT61.D79   1983   649´.8   82-24339
    ISBN 0-87178-030-5

TO RONALD

Acknowledgments

Harvey Varner, R.N., for his dedication and skill, both as student and graduate nurse in caring for Ronald for 18 months in our home; for his valuable contribution to the preparation of the outline for the manuscript; for writing the sections on *Body Mechanics for the Caregiver* and *Moving the Patient up in Bed;* and for his criticism, editing, and suggestions for expanding the text.

Janette M. Oliver, R.N., our daughter, who gave loving support and skilled professional direction both by long distance telephone and during her visits at home; for her instruction and contribution of nursing procedures; for editing and correcting the manuscript.

Robert B. Sullivan, M.D., our family physician, and his assistant, Georgia Beatty, R.N.; Robert E. Fitzgerald, M.D., Urologist, and his medical assistant, Lois Garwood, for their support, their unfailing patience in answering my questions, their prompt attention to telephone calls; for expert advice and superior medical care throughout three years of home care.

Roy W. Day, R.N., and Coralee Poffenroth, R.N., who as student nurses contributed a full measure of skill and compassionate care.

Our daughters, Nyle, Janette, Miriam, and Ann, and their families whose loving concern, support and encouragement never failed us.

Gary Frazier for dedicated care of our yard and trees.

The ministers and members of the First United Methodist Church of Vancouver, Washington, and all other friends who cared and served in innumerable ways to lighten our task.

The American Red Cross for the valuable instruction which I received in their class in Home Nursing in 1942; for assistance which I received from a 1965 edition of the Red

Cross textbook on Home Nursing, to which I have referred both during my home care responsibility and in confirming this text. Now available is the latest edition of the Red Cross textbook, entitled *Family Health and Home Nursing,* Doubleday and Company, Inc., Garden City, New York.

Contents

Part Two

Foreword

Florine Du Fresne's book is not only a "how to" for those who are looking for an alternative to the nursing home, it also gives an inside view of a very loving relationship.

While taking you step-by-step through the events that shaped her husband's last years, this gentle woman displays a strength and courage based simply on her deep and abiding faith in God.

The particulars of home nursing care are covered in an A to Z fashion, while her personal thoughts and feelings are quietly shared. There is no question as to how she copes.

Meeting Mrs. Du Fresne, I was immediately impressed by the depth of her natural sincerity which was reflected in a smile that lights her whole being.

This is a uniquely personal book of straightforward information, for it radiates the joy of devotion, honestly appraises the weariness of carrying through, but rejoices in the comfort and satisfaction that comes from a commitment successfully concluded.

Gelene Hobbs Steudler, R.N., B.S., P.H.N.
Home Care Director
St. Vincent Hospital and Medical Center
Portland, Oregon
President, Oregon Association of
Home Health Agencies—1983

Introduction

An unexpected illness has left someone you love seriously disabled and in need of nursing care. Desiring to do your best to insure his comfort and well-being, you are faced with an important decision. Is an extended care facility the best solution, or can you adequately care for your loved one at home?

Or perhaps an elderly parent, grandparent, or other frail and ailing relative is no longer able to live alone. You want to provide good care with loving, personal attention. The person may have expressed despair at the prospect of being sent to a nursing home. The alternative is home care, but you wonder if you and your family can provide that care.

An increasing number of families are unwilling to leave this responsibility of care to nursing homes. Gradually we are returning to a widening of the family circle to make room for the aged and ill, and to welcome them into a warm and supportive community of love.

Home care is adapted to the emotional and physical needs of the individual. Familiar home environment relieves the fear of being displaced and alleviates the loneliness often experienced in an institution. The aged person who sits alone for long hours, even in his own home, tends to become listless, to neglect eating, and to experience feelings of isolation brought on by sensory deprivation (the insufficient stimulation of sight and hearing, of touch and contact with friends and family). Placed in a familiar environment, the individual participates in the home life and becomes more responsive and communicative. Often appetite improves in ratio to the person's interest in life.

In the home, the caregiver and/or family members quickly notice significant emotional and physical changes in the patient and can take measures to insure relief if necessary. Food is prepared for the patient's nutritional needs and preferences and can be served warm and kept warm during the patient's slow eating.

In contrast to this intimate, personal care is that of the nursing home where high costs, understaffing, patient overload, and the difficulty of finding qualified, sensitive personnel often result in minimal custodial care. No matter how attractive the facility, it is almost impossible to provide the individual with the care that can be given at home.

There are benefits to the family involved in caring for its aged or disabled members. Children willingly help in many ways, and the sensitivity and unselfishness which they acquire in this sharing lasts throughout their lives. The home that is lovingly open to its aged and ill will be a home immeasurably enriched.

I do not pretend that this way is easy or that all the results are positive, but it is a challenge to our love and good will and immensely satisfying to find creative solutions for each other's needs.

Our family has met these crises and we have found many resources for help in solving the practical problems related to home care. It is out of this experience that we hope to help you carry out your responsibilities with confidence, and to be a proficient and effective caregiver.

Six months after the celebration of our 50th wedding anniversary, my husband, Ronald, suffered a brain damaging illness which left him helpless and requiring full-time bed care. As his stay in the hospital was ending, I knew that I could never send him to a nursing home. I rented an electric hospital bed, called an ambulance, and brought him home to begin our great adventure. I have never regretted my decision, and I count these past three years as a rewarding time of growth, of learning, and of satisfaction in fulfilling an important commitment.

About 15 months prior to the onset of Ronald's illness, his 97-year-old mother's near blindness and disabilities of old age made it unsafe for her to live alone any longer in her own home. Her dread of going to a nursing home and the difficulty of finding a live-in companion outweighed her reluctance to leave her home and live with us. Later, even with Ronald's illness, I continued to care for her until her death in our home a few days before her 100th birthday.

The details of home care are as varied as are the persons needing it. Some may be aged relatives, as in the case of Ronald's mother, fiercely independent, able to wait on themselves and to do simple tasks around the house, but needing companionship, a pleasant environment, nourishing meals, and help with personal hygiene. Some are bedfast and helpless. In between is a wide range of disabilities, each requiring unique treatment.

Many of the suggestions and directives I am offering here will apply to any person for whom you are caring at home. Some will apply only to the totally disabled patient. For briefness and clarity, I will refer to the one chiefly responsible for the home care as the *caregiver*, to the supporting assistant as an *aide* or *nurse*, and to the individual needing care as the *patient*.

I have written in outline form so the instructions are easy to follow and identify. Recognizing that home care involves both male and female patients and caregivers, the pronouns "he" and "she" and "him" and "her" are used interchangeably.

Part One

Health Assessment

Doctor's Examination

Upon assuming responsibility for home care ask the patient's doctor to give the patient a thorough physical examination and to report the evaluation and suggestions to you. If the patient has been hospitalized, this information is already available.

Caregiver's Observations

Write in a notebook—a stenographer's notebook will do—your own observations of the patient's condition, even though you may have been seeing her frequently.

1. Observe skin color and tone, and warmth. Are there any breaks in the skin, chapping, flakiness, or clamminess?
2. If the patient has been confined to bed or chair in his own home or in a nursing home, check the pressure areas—buttocks, tail bone, heels, all bony prominences—for decubitus ulcers (bed sores or pressure sores) or for their forerunners, red and tender spots.
3. Is breathing easy and regular, or labored and wheezy?
4. Record temperature, pulse and respiration according to the doctor's instructions. If the patient has a history of high blood pressure, note the doctor's report and ask the doctor how often the blood pressure should be taken. Necessary instructions for these procedures will be included in your orientation by the home health nurse or other qualified person.
5. Observe circulation and mobility. Is the patient able to move freely with or without help? Is there any paralysis? Is there evidence of poor circulation, especially in lower legs and feet? This would be indicated by dark red or blue color in legs and feet, by darkened areas on legs, swelling, or an

an open sore (an ulcer). Is there any swelling of hands and feet or puffiness around the eyes and cheeks? (This is referred to as *edema.*)

6. Is the patient well-fed, overweight, emaciated? Pay particular attention to the appetite, as it can be either an indication of illness or the assurance of well-being. The condition of the body will help indicate the kind and amount of food the patient needs.

7. Body posture:
   a. Is the body straight and relaxed, or twisted and rigid?
   b. Are the hands relaxed and mobile, or are the fingers contracted and curling into the palms of the hands?

8. Ask the mobile patient about the bowel and bladder functions. Is she drinking enough water and other fluids to insure adequate flow or urine? Is there any constipation?
   a. If your patient is confined to bed you can observe output and color of urine. Is it light and clear? If it is scanty, dark, or has a strong odor, increase the intake of fluids.
   b. Observe the condition of the stool (bowel movement), its frequency or irregularity. The stool should be of a firm/ soft consistency. A dry, lumpy, and scanty bowel movement needs correction. A black or tarry stool indicates the presence of old blood and must be reported to the doctor.
   c. Is your patient continent, that is, able to control the flow of urine?
   d. Does the patient have bowel control?

These are important questions because the answers will guide you in protecting bed, clothing, and in regulating diet and medication in cooperation with the doctor. It is especially important to the patient confined to a bed or wheelchair for a long time.

9. It is extremely important to take these assessments. Once you have a detailed knowledge of the patient's general health, you will feel more confident as a caregiver.

Room Space and Equipment Needed

Room

1. The bed patient's room should be on the same floor with the kitchen and living space, if possible, and there should be a toilet and wash bowl on the same level. If the mobile patient has no problem going up and down stairs, a comfortable sleeping room upstairs is acceptable.

2. When our elderly mother came to live with us we converted our den into a room for her. We installed a studio couch, with a sponge rubber pad over the mattress for greater comfort. We left our comfortable chairs in place so that we could share the room with her during the day and early evening. We converted a low cabinet with a table lamp into a stand for her belongings. This arrangement served adequately for many months. When Ronald came home from the hospital, we needed this room for his hospital bed and equipment. We adjusted the furniture in the dining room, placed Grandma's bed in there and made a comfortable nook for her. Our close friends still gathered around our table for dinner or tea and Grandma enjoyed their companionship. This commitment calls for some change in lifestyle. Accepted with good will, life in the home will function smoothly.

3. The patient's room should be bright, with heating and fresh air available. The room occupied by my husband for the three years of his illness had in it the equipment we needed for his care, our television, stereo, book shelves, the pictures of all of our grandchildren, and a bulletin board of snapshots and other memorable events of family life—it was a familiar setting to him.

Equipment

1. The equipment needed depends upon the requirements of

the patient. *For the bedfast invalid,* an all-electric or hand-cranked hospital bed with full-length side rails is preferable. This bed may be raised or lowered to the level convenient for caring for the patient. It facilitates transferring the patient from bed to commode or chair. Some patients may need an attached overhead bar and trapeze.

2. For the very thin patient or the bedfast patient, place a decubitus pad on top of the bed mattress. Most efficient is a wave-cut polyurethane pad, sometimes called an *egg crate mattress.* It is cooler to the skin and relieves the pressure on hips, back and heels. We used a decubitus mattress made in three sections that could be rotated each day to avoid flattening the area under the hips. A sheepskin may give additional comfort.

3. Twin bed size, no-iron sheets, preferably 108 inches long; a minimum of four sheets.

4. Draw or pull sheets. We used twin size sheets, folded hem to hem, for pull sheets. This folded sheet is placed cross-wise over the bottom sheet from about six inches under the pillow to below the hips. It provides a means of turning the patient or moving the patient up or down in the bed.

5. Foam rubber pillows for under head and shoulders and for propping the back and legs. We also used washable baby crib pillows for under hands and arms when needed. A supply of pillow slips.

6. Disposable, moisture repellent Chux, purchased at the pharmacy, are convenient protection for the bed. The Chux should not be left for long periods of time under the patient, as they cause overheating of the skin, moisture, and will contribute to the onset of decubitus ulcers.

7. A lightweight thermal blanket will usually provide enough warmth and is easy to wash and dry. We also used white sheet-blankets, in cold weather placing one over the patient, next to the body, and under the top sheet; in warm weather, over the top sheet as a lightweight blanket. Old sheet blankets cut in different sized squares also provide soft cloths for many uses.

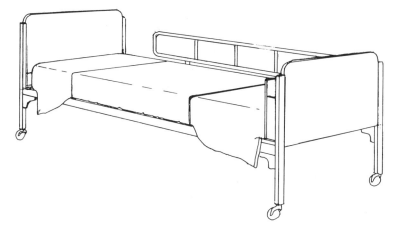

A draw or pull sheet provides a means of moving the patient up or down in the bed.

8.   Several soft, lightweight bath towels and washcloths. For the bedfast patient, finger towels a size larger than a washcloth make excellent washcloths. Enough of these articles should be provided for convenience in laundering. Many of them may already be in the home.

9.   A bedside stand is convenient for placing a tray, a glass of water, or the patient's personal articles within reach.

10.   Toilet articles, including an electric shaver for the man, a good mild soap, deodorant, denture or dental care items, a good lotion for the skin (such as Vaseline Intensive Care Lotion, Keri Lotion, or a similar mild cream), and cotton balls.

11.   For the bedfast patient, an adjustable over-bed table may be used for meals, or for putting books, equipment and materials within reach.

12.   A kidney-shaped basin to use for oral care, and a plastic or rubber-made tub or pan, about 10 inches by 12 inches and approximately 6 inches deep.

13.   A bedpan, if this is needed, and two urinals of the plastic

type, for convenience in emptying and measuring. There is a functional female urinal which would be easier to use than a bedpan.

14. The commode: If your patient is unable to walk to the bathroom easily or it is difficult to position the patient on the toilet, provide a commode which may be placed when needed beside the bed or chair for easy transfer. The commode is a chair, sometimes on wheels, with back, arms and a toilet seat under which is a plastic catch basin. The seat of the commode should be padded for comfort and for the protection of bony hips. We made an inexpensive seat pad with a square of 4-inch-thick foam rubber, cut and trimmed to fit the opening in the toilet seat. This pad may be protected from soil by a long, folded strip of outing flannel or other soft cloth which can be removed for laundering. An old, solid chair may be converted into a commode.

15. If your patient is unable to walk alone or with a cane or a walker, a wheelchair may be needed. Wheelchairs are available in different sizes and styles, depending on the patient's needs. A walker provides safe support for the person who is learning to walk again, or who has some paralysis, or who loses balance easily. For some patients a strong cane is all that is necessary for security. These, too, are made in several styles and sizes, including a 4-pronged footed cane.

16. For the bedfast patient who can give some assistance in a transfer, a sliding board is helpful. You can make one by using 5/8-inch-thick veneer, 9 by 24 inches, with rounded corners. Sand well and finish with enough coats of varnish or Valspar to create a smooth surface. This board may be placed between the bed and chair, or between a chair and the bath bench in the bathtub to permit an easy transfer for the patient.

17. A bath bench with a back provides safety and comfort for the person who can be helped into the bathtub or shower, but who finds it difficult or unsafe to stand in the tub or to sit down in the water and get up again.

18. Provide a rubber mat or other nonslip surface in the tub or

shower. Hand grips in the tub or shower are also important. Be sure that bath mats cannot slip.

19. A flexible tube with a shower head may be attached to either the fixed overhead shower head, or to the bathtub faucet by using an adapter. It is a convenient appliance for the patient sitting on the bath bench or who needs help in taking a shower or bath. Don't forget the shower cap.

20. If your patient is helpless and unable to assist herself, a patient lift is a great help in transferring her from bed to wheelchair and back. The patient lift is a hydraulic lift with a choice of sling types, according to the patient's need. The patient who is paralyzed but who can follow directions and offer some assistance can more easily be moved, even to the commode. (This move to the commode by the lift is not possible for a totally helpless patient who becomes rigid and unable to relax.) The lift will save the back of the nurse and caregiver, and also makes the transfer safer and easier for the most helpless patient.

21. For the infirm or elderly person in your home, provide a comfortable chair with a supportive back and arms, and an upholstered hassock or footstool about the same height as the chair seat. It is important that when the older person, or a person with circulatory problems, is seated, to always elevate the feet and legs with good support. Set in a pleasant, draft-free spot.

22. In Appendix A, page 100, I suggest sources for obtaining these various items as needed, whether you have the financial means to rent or purchase them, or need financial assistance.

Securing Adequate Help in the Home

Additional help in the home will probably not be necessary when an elderly patient is able to take care of most personal needs. You may wish to find a reliable person whom you can ask to stay with your family member for a few hours if you need to leave home and do not want the person to stay alone.

For the helpless bedfast patient, good assistance will be needed. Our first need when bringing our patient home from the hospital was that of nursing assistance. I could do the procedures needed for his bed care, but I could not lift him alone, nor transfer him from bed to chair and back again. Neither was I alone able to assume around-the-clock turning, bathing, and all that was needed to make him comfortable.

We called our community college school of nursing and they sent to us a young man, Harvey, who had completed his first year of nurse's training. For the first year of Ronald's illness and for half of the third year, after Harvey had graduated, he helped us for four hours a day in a split shift, which we adjusted to his class schedule. During the second year he trained, at different times, two other students who took his place when he was no longer available.

Harvey was dedicated and capable. I shared with him the training I had received in a Red Cross Home Nursing course which I had taken during World War II. He taught me everything he was learning about patient care in the school of nursing. We shared responsibility, consulted often, and devised new procedures in problem solving. If we failed in one, we tried another. Together, he and I, and the students who followed him, gave our patient the best care possible.

Nursing Assistance
1. Contact the school of nursing in your community regard-

ing availability of student nurses.

2. Hospitals sometimes keep a registry of aides and licensed vocational nurses who want part-time work or who want extra hours in addition to their full-time hospital employment.

3. There are professional home-help agencies who can provide screened assistants for home care, either part-time or full-time. Their skills may range from those of Registered Nurses (RN's) through Licensed Vocational Nurses (LVN's) and nurse's aides, to homemakers who can prepare nutritious meals, do light housework, and provide some free time for the primary caregiver.

4. In our community, the Southwest Washington Health District's Home Health Agency has a division of Home Nursing. Upon request from the attending physician, the agency will send a Registered Nurse to the home to evaluate the needs of the patient and make recommendations. If medical or nursing procedures which can legally be performed only by a Registered Nurse are prescribed by your doctor, the agency will provide these services in the home. During short-term need, the agency will send an aide to the home to give the patient a bed bath. This is a help with a short-term patient who is recuperating from surgery or illness, or in an emergency.

5. If you have had no experience or training in home nursing, such a community agency will send a qualified person to the home to teach you how to care for your patient. The cost of these services is covered by Medicare or Medicaid according to existing guidelines. If the patient is not eligible for either of these financial helps, or has no private insurance, there is a nominal charge for such services.

Other Assistance

1. If your patient is capable of self-help and is responsible for most needs, you may need only the help of a caring person who can come to the home one or two times a week to free the primary caregiver for an afternoon or evening. Or you may need someone to help with housework, laundry, and patient care for a few hours a week.

2. We did not overlook offers of help from friends in our neighborhood or church family. Often the church or service club to which you belong provides volunteers who are glad to do errands for you when you cannot leave the house, or who will sit with your patient while you do the shopping or get out for a needed break. We learned to accept gladly the help offered by friends. We were careful not to impose on the same people all the time, but called on different friends when we needed help. However, our friend and neighbor across the street came every evening at 9 for two years to help me position my patient for the first half of the night, a turn which was difficult for me to make alone. He continued to come every week on the evening of our live-in nurse's day off. Not only was the physical help important but the few minutes of friendly exchange cheered us immeasurably.

   The caregiver receiving such help can find ways of saying "Thank you"—a plate of cookies, a gift, tickets to a concert, or dinner out, or in the home, for those who help.

   I did not try to carry out all the responsibility alone. Family, friends, all who came and went, were a blessing. It is also a blessing to friends who help, and gives them the satisfaction of meeting a need and the opportunity to share concern for a friend. None of us lives to ourselves alone.

3. Every community has volunteer agencies or projects for helping handicapped or elderly people. Possible agencies and their functions are listed in Appendix A, page 100.

4. The primary caregiver should make arrangements at times for extra live-in help so that she may leave home for a few days at a time for rest and change, in addition to the short breaks during the week. This is practical and necessary if she is to maintain good health and well-being during what may be a long commitment.

The Role of the Nurse in Home Care

The condition of the patient and the ability of the home caregiver will indicate the type of nursing care needed and for how many hours per day. We gave the best of care with not more than four hours of nursing help each day, preferably in a split shift. Occasionally, circumstances made it necessary for me to work alone for a day or more. Then I could draw upon my volunteer help if needed.

1. The nurse, whether student or experienced aide, will give not only skilled, professional care to the patient, but will advise and teach the home caregiver and other family members the correct procedures. The sharing of responsibilities by family members is desirable and important.
2. The nurse is answerable to the home caregiver and to the doctor. He or she should always be given full cooperation, courtesy and appreciation.
3. Discuss the patient's condition and necessary procedures plainly with the nurse, especially those parts of the care for which you will be responsible when the nurse is not on duty. If your nurse is a student or even an experienced aide, do not take for granted that everything is being done according to your direction and with correct procedures. Know the procedures yourself. Be courteous and kind, but insist that the standards set and the instructions given by the training personnel be carefully observed. Be just as careful in following the instructions yourself.
4. In the case of terminal illness, if you and your patient and the family have agreed not to use extraordinary measures to prolong life, the nurse should be informed. In the event of a crisis occurring in your absence, the nurse will be able to proceed according to your instructions, knowing that you will assume all responsibility.

The Role of the Doctor in Home Care

When assuming responsibility for home care, inform the person's doctor and, as is suggested in the section entitled *Health Assessment,* page 21, ask for the doctor's assessment and recommendations. Use the following guidelines to help his instructions be more effective.

1. *NEVER* give any medication, even aspirin, or apply heat, ice, ointment, or other materials without orders from the doctor or his nurse.

   a. Do not ask your pharmacist to supply remedies without the doctor's orders. Your doctor will tell you what treatment or medication you can use at your own discretion or under given circumstances, so that ordinarily you will not have to consult him unless a condition develops in which you are uncertain.

2. Keep your doctor informed if there is any unusual symptom or a change in the patient's condition. He will usually advise you by telephone, but try to avoid unnecessary telephone calls. Your judgment and decision-making will improve with practice.

3. If it is necessary to consult the doctor, give him the information correctly and concisely without offering your opinions.

   a. Tell him what you actually see: temperature; pulse; blood pressure, if it is customary to keep this record, or if the blood pressure has been taken; the patient's color; any vomiting; bowel irregularity; urine output and fluid intake.

   b. You cannot see pain and nausea. The correct way to report these symptoms is to say, "The patient is complaining of severe pain in the lower abdomen," or "of persistent headache," or "of nausea." The doctor will evaluate this condition.

c. Report accurately, in as few words as possible, what you see and what the patient complains of. We will discuss later the keeping of a daily chart which you can use when reporting to the doctor.

Patient Care and Hygiene

Preparation of the Bed

1. When the bed is empty:
   a. If the mattress of the hospital bed is protected with a plastic cover, tuck over it an old sheet to absorb moisture from condensation of body heat.
   b. Over this old sheet place the decubitus mattress pad.
   c. Cover the decubitus mattress pad with the clean bottom sheet. Tuck this sheet only under the head and foot of the mattress. Leave sides free to permit air circulation.
   d. Place the pull sheet (see page 24 for description) across the bed so that it extends from about six inches under the head pillow to the knees. We found it necessary to tuck the ends of this sheet in firmly under the mattress to prevent its bunching and wrinkling under the patient when turning or bringing the patient up in bed. This will still permit enough air circulation from the remaining untucked areas.
   e. Fan-fold the top sheet across the foot of the bed, leaving the top end free to pull up over the patient. Place the folded blanket across the foot of the bed and the pillow at the head of the bed. Keep within reach another pillow for propping the back.
2. Changing the sheets and pull sheet with the patient in the bed will be described at the conclusion of bathing instructions.

The Bath

1. The care of the patient's skin is of the utmost importance. The bedfast patient should have a full bed bath every day. soap and water may be used one day, and on the alternate

days use a good skin lotion and water. Lotion should be applied with a washcloth, in the same manner as soap. The condition of the skin will be the guide. If the skin is dry and flaky, wash with lotion and water on alternate days. Fill the bath pan or tub with temperature-tested warm water and place on a stand within convenient reach. Explain to the patient what you are going to do during each step of the bath. If the patient is impaired mentally, she may be easily startled or upset by a sudden movement or an unexpected procedure.

2. The caregiver or nurse must always thoroughly wash her hands with soap and warm water, rinse and dry, before caring for the patient at any time. Keep clean towels and soap beside the bathroom bowl for this purpose. When patient care is completed, the nurse should again wash her hands. This prevents the spread of bacteria from nurse to patient and from patient to nurse.

3. Before starting the bath, warm the room and collect all of the equipment needed and place it on a stand within easy reach. This will include washcloths, towels, soap, skin lotion, deodorant, supplies for care of tooth. Clean clothing, sheets, pull sheets and pillow covers should be placed in order of use on a chair or table near the bed.

4. Shaving: The male patient may shave himself either before or after the bath, or if he is unable to do so, he may be shaved by the caregiver. Use an electric razor. Do not use shaving lotions, unless there is a special reason, because they contain alcohol which dries the skin. If the man has been accustomed to shaving every day, continue this routine. He will be more comfortable if cleanshaven. Clean the razor after each use, according to the instructions given with the razor. Elderly women sometimes have a growth of facial hair. When caring for herself a well-groomed woman either plucks or shaves the hair. When she is ill, she should be asked by the caregiver if she would like to have the chin and surrounding area shaved. She may be able to do this herself if given a mirror and an electric razor. Otherwise, she will be grateful for the caregiver's thoughtfulness. A woman rarely loses her desire to look her best.

5. Oral Care: This may also be given before the bath or afterward. We found it easier to give it before the bath.
   a. Instructions for care of teeth will be given in the section entitled, *Oral Care,* page 52.
   b. For either shaving the patient or brushing the teeth, bring the patient to an upright position in the bed. Raise the bed level to its highest position.
6. Remove the blanket and top sheet and cover the patient with a lightweight bath blanket, such as a sheet blanket.
7. Turn the patient on her back and bring the body into good alignment if she is unable to do this unaided.
8. Use the following bathing procedures.
   a. Raise the bed to its highest level. Lower the head of the bed so that the patient is lying almost flat. Place a towel under the patient's head to protect the pillow.
   b. Use two washcloths, one for applying soap or lotion and water, the other for rinsing. This method lessens accumulations of soap in the water.
   c. Wash the patient's face with soap and water, and on alternate days with warm water and lotion. Be gentle, washing away from the corners of the eyes, and around the mouth and nose. Carefully wash the area inside the fold of the external ear and behind the ears. This area, and that of the eyebrows if they are heavy, will collect a moist deposit of old skin, cream and soap. If not carefully cleaned, rinsed and dried, this will cause red, irritated, scaly patches. Never clean the ear canal with a Q-Tip or any similar instrument. Rinse the face and pat dry.
   d. Wash the neck as far back as you can reach. The back of the neck can be washed when washing the patient's back.
   e. To protect the bed, tuck a bath towel under the patient's side from the shoulder to the hip on the near side. Pull the bath blanket down to the abdomen.
   f. Soap, rinse, and dry the chest and sides of the chest, using a firm but gentle touch. Wash and dry the area under the breasts of the female patient. Cover the

chest with a clean towel.

g. Wash the abdomen and lower sides of abdomen, upper thighs and pubic area. Rinse and dry. Avoid pressure. Pull up the blanket.

h. Change the water. Leave the towel under the patient's near arm and shoulder. Soap, rinse and dry the arm and the underarm, always supporting the arm and using firm, gentle pressure. Wash upward from wrist to shoulder to stimulate circulation. Wash the hand, separating the fingers. Pay special attention to the palm; loose skin and soapy deposits will collect there. Be sure to dry the palm of the hand and between the fingers thoroughly.

i. If it is possible to place the pan containing a small amount of warm water on the bed, wash the patient's hand in the pan. This is pleasant and relaxing.

j. Place a bath towel under the far arm and hand. Repeat procedures h and i. Remove the damp towels. Apply underarm deodorant (not a spray).

k. Help the patient flex the knee nearest you. Place a towel under the buttock, the leg and foot. Cover the other leg with a towel. Wash, rinse, and dry the leg and foot, using long, firm strokes. Repeat on far leg. If the patient's legs are hairy, use only clear water on them every other day because the hair tends to collect soap residue. Dry thoroughly between the toes. If the patient's feet become dry and scaly, massage some lotion into the feet and between the toes. If the feet sweat and feel moist, dust the feet and between the toes with cornstarch. Examine the feet carefully, as you care for them, for any rough areas, red patches or sores. Examine the heels, as they are a critical area for pressure sores.

l. Change the water. At this time if the patient is able to do so, have him or her wash the genital area with soap and water. Rinse and dry well. If the patient is helpless the caregiver or nurse must give the care. Be gentle and thorough.

    (1) If the patient is an uncircumcised male, retract

the foreskin. Rinse and dry with gentle patting rather than rubbing. Bring the foreskin down again over the glans.

(2) Watch for any signs of redness, irritation, blisters, or other skin problems which may come from dampness, bladder infection, or urine burn.

(3) If the scrotum is dry and flaky, gently apply a small amount of lotion, but not often enough to cause moisture and oiliness. If there is any redness around the genitals or between the buttocks, dust with cornstarch and a soft cloth. Inform the doctor if you see any swelling or hardness in the testicles, or if the patient complains of pain and soreness with the most gentle touch or pressure.

(4) If your patient is a woman, carefully wash the folds and crevices which comprise the genital area. It is not enough just to wash over the pubic area with soap and water. The proper procedure is to separate the external folds (the labia), expose the folds and crevices which form the vulva, the opening of the urethra, and all surrounding soft tissue. Be very gentle. Carefully wash all of these parts with a warm, soapy, soft cloth, rinsing and drying thoroughly. If these inner folds are not washed twice a day, an odorous, white deposit will collect there and will be a source of bacteria buildup, and of burning itching and redness. If the patient is helpless, she may not be able to complain about the discomfort. Even if the patient is able to wash the area herself, give her the necessary instructions and check to see that the cleansing is properly done.

(5) If there is evidence of redness and soreness it may help to wash the area with Peri-Wash, a medicated, healing, liquid soap. Follow the directions on the tube or jar. If the area is kept clean and dry, a mild soap will be sufficient.

(6) An elderly woman frequently dribbles urine

which is irritating to the tender tissues when it is allowed to remain for hours. While the patient is on the bedpan, it is helpful to pour a glass of warm water over the area and pat dry after urination. If you are keeping a record of intake and output of fluids, note how many cc's of water the glass holds, then subtract that amount from the urine measurement.

(7) Check between the folds of the buttocks for any sign of redness, rash, or chapping, especially if the woman has heavy thighs. Keep skin off skin by placing an old, soft pillow slip or similar old soft cloth between the thighs, wrapping the pillow around one thigh to prevent its slipping off.

(8) If the patient is heavy and has a fold of abdominal flesh which sags over the pubic area, wash, rinse and dry the skin under the fold and separate the fold of flesh from the body with an old soft cloth. It is easier to prevent chapping and irritation than to heal it.

(9) If the genital area develops more aggravated redness and rawness use Sween Cream, which promotes healing and is made by the makers of Peri-Wash. This is an excellent cream but should be used only in the event of a problem. Make sure before applying cornstarch or any powder around the area or between the buttocks that the skin is cleansed and completely dry and then apply only a light dusting. After the patient has urinated, wash the area with warm water and pat dry. The use of bathroom tissue is insufficient. This is care that is often neglected, resulting in much discomfort. If you should see an unusual sign of irritation and soreness, notify your doctor or the visiting nurse and get instructions for its care.

(10) Keeping the area clean and dry, and preventing skin touching skin will usually prevent any irritation or chapping.

m. Change the bath water again.

n. Ask the patient to turn on her far side with her back toward you. If she is unable to turn unaided, then you will make the turn. Ask the patient to hold the raised side rail with the up-hand. Tuck a dry towel under her down-side, the full length of the back from the shoulder to the buttocks. Wash the back of the neck, the shoulders, and down the back. Work toward the buttocks. Be sure to wash well between the buttocks. Rinse and dry well, beginning at the neck and working down the back. Examine the back for any signs of redness or tenderness.

o. Using lotion, give a good back rub. Use firm pressure with both the heel of the hand and the fingers in a smooth, circular massage, stimulating the circulation and rubbing in the lotion. Use both hands.

p. Expect the patient to help with the bath and the moving in bed to the extent that the patient is able to follow instructions and to move her body. Some bed-fast patients are able to bathe themselves except for the back and some areas like the feet which are hard to reach. This is stimulating to the patient and better than to wait on her throughout the bath. The care-giver should always be present to help and to check the skin for any signs of redness.

Making the Bed with the Patient in the Bed

1. If the patient cannot be moved at this time from the bed to a chair, then the bottom sheet and the pull sheet should be changed with the patient in bed, using the following procedure:

   a. Leave the patient on her side, facing the far side of bed and holding the rail.

   b. Tuck the soiled bottom sheet and draw sheet length-wise to the center of the bed and as far as possible under the patient.

   c. Place the clean sheet lengthwise on the bed with the midfold at the center of the bed and the near-half smoothly over the near side of the bed, as if the bed were half made.

d. Lay the pull sheet on top of the bottom sheet in the same way, with the midfold at the center of the bed and in correct position to extend from six inches under the head pillow to a little below the knees of the patient.

e. Fold the far half of the sheet and pull sheet in a fanlike fold, tucking it as close to the folded soiled linen as possible. Tuck the head and foot of the near half of the clean sheet under the near half of the mattress at the head and foot of the bed to hold it firmly.

f. Explain to the patient that you are going to turn her toward you and that for a moment she will feel that she is rolling over a long ridge of the folded sheets. Loosen patient's grip on the rail.

g. Then turn the patient toward you in this manner: Place your feet about eight inches apart with one foot in front of the other. Bend over as close to the patient's body as possible. Place your arm, from elbow to hand, behind the patient's shoulder and along the body, and the other hand and arm behind the hips. Use your thighs and legs, rather than your back to control the turn and hold the weight, then turn the patient toward you in one steady, smooth movement, bringing the patient over the roll of soiled and clean linen.

h. Supporting the patient's back with your hand, reach behind the patient and pull out the roll of soiled linen and pull through the fanned clean linen.

i. At this point, ask the patient to hold the raised, near bedrail for support while you go to the other side of the bed. Pull all of the linen smoothly into place and complete tucking the bottom sheet under the mattress at the head and the foot of the bed. Pull the draw sheet tight and smooth and tuck as instructed under the mattress. A tall person can do this procedure from one side of the bed, but it will be necessary for a shorter person to work from both sides of the bed. Use this method at any time when it is necessary to change wet or soiled linen.

2. If it is possible for the patient to be up in a chair or wheel-chair, or to use the commode, change the bed linen while the patient is out of the bed.

Dressing the Patient

1. Help the patient put on clean clothing, whether a shirt or gown.

   a. For the helpless bedfast patient, use minimum clothing, for ease in turning and handling. For our patient we used an attractive white or colored pullover or button-down-the front style T-shirt, the same shirt he would have worn for casual dress had he been well. We did not use underwear or pajama bottoms. This clothing is impractical for an incontinent patient who is using a catheter or urinal. Also, the genital area needs as much air and freedom as possible to keep it dry and free from sweating.

   b. For the woman bed patient, an attractive short gown and perhaps a bed jacket will be sufficient.

Positioning the Patient in Bed

1. After the bath it will be time for the patient to rest. The bedfast patient tends to curl up in bed, lying with legs drawn up, elbows bent, hands clenched. Whatever the reasons for this posture, it is important, especially if the patient is lying on her side, to keep the patient's body in good alignment, with head, back and hips in a straight line, and knees slightly flexed.

2. The back should be supported from shoulder to hips by a pillow folded lengthwise and tucked firmly under the down-side of the patient.

3. Place a soft pillow between the patient's knees, and a small, soft pillow between the feet. If the patient is immobile and unable to shift position without help, place another small pillow under the up-arm, seeing that the hand is also comfortably supported.

4. Adjust the head pillow so that the neck and head are both supported, whether the patient is lying on her side or back.

5. Elevate the head of the bed slightly.

6. The immobile patient often resists being moved and will protest any change of position. Be gentle but firm. Joints and muscles held in a tense, rigid position for any length of time eventually will contract and can be moved only with great discomfort to the patient. But they must be moved, straightened, and their position changed frequently. Encourage the patient to relax during any move. Contractures are painful and all possible care should be taken to prevent them.

7. Do not leave a pillow under the knees of the patient when the patient is lying on her back. This will impair circulation, risking the danger of blood clot. Instead, place a pillow just above the knees, and another pillow slightly below the knees. This is one of the values of small pillows or soft, rolled towels.

8. To successfully move your patient without injury to yourself or to the patient, it is important to understand and practice good body mechanics. These instructions are given next before proceeding to other areas of care.

Body Mechanics for the Caregiver

Body mechanics have been described as the efficient use of the body as a machine and as a means for locomotion. Good health depends on how carefully and efficiently we utilize our body parts in relationship to internal and external forces.

The importance of understanding body mechanics is universal for everyone whether healthy or ill. We should use good body mechanics in every phase of our daily activities. Good body mechanics are not accomplished by following a set procedure. They are best described as a set of actions that maintain the body in positions and postures that promote optimum movement and functioning.

Basic Principles

1. Maintain a good body posture during all daily activities: feet pointing forward about eight inches apart, knees extended but relaxed, the abdomen held up and the rib cage raised and held erect. Good posture is essential in all positions: sitting, standing, or lying down. Do not slump!
2. When feeding your patient or reading to him, sit with your hips against the back of the chair, body erect, shoulders relaxed. You will not tire so quickly.
3. Whenever moving your patient—for example, turning him in the bed—keep your body in good alignment.
4. Tighten abdominal and arm muscles for action, and bring your patient close to your body as directed in making a good turn.
5. By using good body mechanics and the principles of mechanical laws, moving and lifting helpless patients can be made relatively easy. It is essential that the nurse and the caregiver understand such procedures and have seen them demonstrated so that you are not entirely dependent

upon help from others. Never lift more than you can comfortably handle. If you are alone and it is necessary to move the patient in a way you cannot manage comfortably, call someone in to help or wait until the assigned assistant comes. If the family is taught how to move the patient correctly, home care is accepted more readily.

Moving the Patient Up in Bed, One-Person Method

1. Always raise the bed to its highest position before moving the patient. Lower the head of the bed. Children and lightweight adults are relatively easy to slide toward the head of the bed without assistance. Average weights of 140 to 150 pounds pose a problem except for the male nurse or a tall and strong woman. (As I copy our nurse's instructions for this area of care, I must say that I, and most other women weighing 115 pounds or less and who are senior citizens, would not be able to move a person weighing 140 pounds. This is a procedure for which you must know your strength and not go beyond it.) Turning the patient in bed as directed can be done safely, but for lifting up, or moving the patient up in bed, get help. Use the principles of good body mechanics as described.

2. The head of the bed must always be placed in the flat position before moving a patient up in bed with the patient on his back. NEVER TRY TO MOVE A PATIENT UP-HILL. If the patient is capable of assisting, ask him to place his hands on his chest and keep them there during the move. If the patient is not responsive, the nurse or caregiver must position the hands on the chest and firmly press them in place. Usually the patient will leave them there.

3. For the lighter weight patient, face the side of the patient nearest you and place your hands under the patient's armpits. Bring yourself directly over the patient, keep your body in good alignment, and using your arm muscles—not your back muscles—gently push the patient up in bed. If the patient can assist, ask him to bring the legs up and push against the mattress with his feet when you make the move. Just this much pushing on the part of the pa-

tient helps relieve the strain on the caregiver.

Moving the Patient Up in Bed, Two-Person Method

1. If the patient is unable to assist by pushing with his feet, the nurse and assistant will need to hold him so that the heaviest part of the body is moved by them and not by the patient. It may be easier to flex the patient's knees and hold them in place with a pillow. Place a pillow against the head of the bed.

2. The persons stand at either side of the bed, facing each other at a point between the patient's waist and hips. Both persons give themselves a wide base of support, feet well apart, knees flexed. Leaning close to the patient, they join hands under the widest part of the patient's hips and shoulders.

3. On the count of three, both of them rock toward the head of the bed and slide the patient up in bed. This procedure may need to be repeated if the patient is heavy and/or far down in the bed. Care should be taken to avoid injury to the patient's neck and head.

Using a Draw Sheet to Move the Patient Up in the Bed

1. Place a pillow against the head of the bed. The nurse and assistant stand at opposite sides of the bed at a point near the patient's shoulders and chest, and *facing the foot of the bed.*

2. Roll the sides of the draw sheet, which extends under the patient from under the head to below the buttocks, toward the patient from either side so that they may be easily grasped. Ask the patient to relax and not to offer any resistance to the movement.

3. The caregivers place their feet to form a wide base of support with the leg nearest the bed behind, and the other leg in front. Holding the rolled draw sheet securely at (a) a point near the patient's neck and (b) at the lumbar region, they first lean forward and rock backward. As they rock backward, the weight of their bodies helps to slide the draw sheet and the patient up in the bed. At the completion of the rocking motion each caregiver usually has his

elbow nearest the patient, on the mattress. This procedure can be done with the caregivers facing the head of the bed, but it seems easier when the backward rock is used. In the forward rock, there seems to be a certain amount of upward pull necessary.

4. The nurse and the caregiver can usually make this move. If the patient is extremely heavy, only an hydraulic patient lift should be used.

Transferring the Patient from Bed to Chair and Back

1. This procedure will be discussed in connection with transferring the patient to the commode. It is a procedure for which the nurse will have had professional instruction, and hopefully, some experience. If the patient is helpless, tends to be rigid, and weighs 125 pounds or more, the nurse and/or caregiver must be tall enough and strong enough to make the pivot transfer without injury to his back and legs, or he must have help. I never attempted a pivot transfer alone, but I usually was present to help with positioning our patient's arms, to see that his feet were flat on the floor, or to move the commode behind him so that the nurse could seat him properly.

2. The instructions for such a transfer are not given in this book because they must be demonstrated several times on a one-to-one basis by the person who gives the home training.

More on Patient Hygiene

Additional Care of Hands and Feet

1. Trim fingernails when necessary, using manicuring scissors. Smooth the edges with a file or emery board. Long fingernails can cause scratches or abrasions.

2. A woman patient may take pride in the appearance of her hands. If she wishes, apply her preferred fingernail polish. Poor vision or tremor may prevent her caring for her nails herself.

3. If the patient is immobile, paralyzed, or tends to be rigid, the fingers may contract into the palms of the hands. Eventually, they cannot be unbent without pain and the contracture itself is painful. Passive exercise will help correct this condition, and these instructions will be given later.

    a. Roll a small towel or similar piece of cloth into a hand grip about three inches in diameter and place in the patient's hand. Our patient held his hand grips most of the time, helping to maintain a degree of flexibility. This cloth should be changed daily for laundering.

4. The feet require careful attention.

    a. Trim the toenails with scissors or clippers, cutting the nails straight across. Smooth edges with emery board or file.

    b. If the corners of the large toe turn down into the flesh, carefully work a small piece of absorbent cotton under the toenail with an orangewood stick, beginning at the corner of the toenail. Do not press too hard.

    c. Give a footbath when the patient is sitting in a chair or on the commode. Protect the floor with a towel and place the patient's feet in a pan of warm, soapy water. Let the feet soak for a while, then remove the soapy water, fill the pan with clear, warm water, and rinse and dry the feet. Dry well between toes. This is a pleasant, soothing treatment for the feet.

d. *Foot-drop* occurs in a long-term bedfast patient who is unable to walk or stand, unless special care is taken to prevent it. If even lightweight covers are permitted to lie on the patient's feet when she is on her back, the muscles and tendons which support the feet will eventually lose their tone and the feet will drop into a dangling position, over which the patient will have no control.

   (1) When covering the patient, be sure to make a lengthwise pleat with the sheet and blanket together to loosen covers over the feet, and lift the fold up to keep the weight of the covers off the feet.

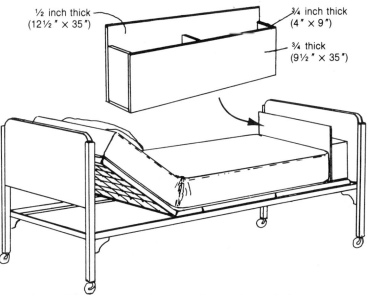

½ inch thick (12½ " × 35")

¾ inch thick (4" × 9")

¾ thick (9½ " × 35")

A boxlike construction can be made to help prevent foot-drop.

(2) The most effective protection against foot-drop is a piece of one-half-inch plywood, cut as long as the bed is wide. When placed on the springs of the bed at the foot of the mattress, it stands up five or six inches above the toes. Cover the board with an old, folded sheet blanket or other soft, washable material. The covers will hang over the board and will not touch the feet when the patient is lying on her back.

(3) Also, the patient can press her feet against the board, giving them support and helping to keep them in correct position. If the patient is able to assist in moving herself up in bed, she can push against the footboard and make the move easier.

If there is too much space between the footboard and the mattress, use a boxlike construction instead of a single board. (See illustration.)

Care of Hair

1. The patient's hair can be shampooed when the patient is sitting up in a chair or on the commode. Our patient's hair was heavy and oily and needed shampooing about every five days. The condition of the patient and of the hair will be a guide to the frequency of the shampoo.

2. Place a tub of warm water, two washcloths, shampoo, and clean towels within easy reach on a table. Drape the patient with a large bath towel and explain what you are going to do.

3. Moisten the hair thoroughly with a washcloth and warm water.

4. Apply the shampoo and massage well into the hair, being careful to keep the soap away from the patient's eyes.

5. Wipe off the lather with the washcloth, rinsing it out in the pan of water. Then, using clean water and the rinsing cloth, apply the cloth to the hair while wet but not dripping. Squeeze out in pan. Repeat, changing the water as often as necessary, until the rinsing water is free of soap.

6. Partially dry the hair with a clean towel. Then finish dry-

ing with a warm blow-dryer if one is available, combing the hair into shape.

7. This same procedure can be used for a woman patient, but if her hair is long, one may need to use a professional shampoo basin, or drape a large plastic cover around the patient's shoulders, covered with a towel. Place a small table or stand behind the chair and secure the plastic and towel to the table so that water does not drip onto the floor. Place the pan of warm water on the stand and let the patient's hair hang over the water.

8. Use the method described in steps 3 through 6 for shampooing the hair of a patient in bed. Remove the pillow. Place a small Chux, covered by a bath towel, under the patient's head. Elevate the head of the bed for ease in washing the hair.

9. Occasionally our patient's hair was cut by his barber, who came to the house. But the haircut or set can also be given by the caregiver or nurse.

The Bath for the Ambulatory Patient

So far we have discussed only the procedures for bathing the bedfast patient. Many elderly or infirm patients can bathe themselves with some assistance.

1. Warm the bathroom. Help the patient, if necessary, to lay out towels, washcloth, shower cap, clean clothing, or any other needed equipment.

2. Provide nonslip, secure footing in the tub or shower, and a bath mat that will not slip.

3. Test the temperature of the water in the tub or shower.

4. The patient may need to sit on a bath bench during the shower or bath. If it is difficult for her to get into the tub and out, use the sliding board. Set one end of the board securely on a chair beside the tub, and the other end securely on the bath bench. Cover the board with a small towel to make sliding easier.

5. Drape the chair beside the tub with a bath towel.

6. After the patient has given herself as much of the bath as possible, she may need help with washing her back.

7. Help the patient out of the tub and onto the chair. Give

any assistance needed in drying, especially the back and feet which are sometimes hard for an older person to reach.

8. If a daily tub or shower requires more effort than the patient feels able to exert, cover a chair beside the bathroom bowl, using a large towel. Help the patient take a sponge bath. Give any assistance needed and offer to wash and dry the back. In this way, one tub bath or shower per week may be sufficient. If the woman patient is elderly she may need a reminder to wash the genital area daily with soap and water.

9. Give your patient a good back rub with lotion before she dresses and puts on her gown. A back rub is relaxing and restful.

10. This care should be adapted to the degree of capability and needs of the mobile patient. It is important to make the bath time pleasant. Be patient. We need to realize that age and impairment may eventually bring us to a place of such dependence. We need to think how we will feel if we are dependent upon another person for these very personal services.

Oral Care

1. Follow this procedure when the patient has natural teeth.

   a. Place within easy reach of the bed: a soft toothbrush, toothpaste, possibly baking soda or other dentifrice, a glass of warm water, dental floss if desired, and the kidney-shaped basin. Bring patient to an upright position.

   b. Provide these items twice a day and encourage the patient to clean the teeth well, rinse the mouth several times and spit the water into the basin. Mouthwash is optional. Provide a small towel for drying around the mouth. Rinse the toothbrush, wipe it on a towel or tissue and place it with the brush up in a holder or glass so that it can dry and air.

   c. If the patient is unable to clean her teeth, then the

caregiver or nurse should encourage the patient's cooperation. Ask the patient to open her mouth, explaining what you are going to do. Gently brush the front and back teeth up and down. Include two or three soft strokes the length of the tongue to remove any accumulation of mucus or food residue. After brushing, offer the patient warm water to swish in her mouth, then hold the basin well under the chin so that the patient can spit the water out. Repeat until the water is clear. Dry around the mouth.

d. If the patient is unable to cooperate or respond well to directions, she may resist by biting down on the brush, closing the mouth tightly, or spitting out the toothpaste. Be patient. Speak gently and quietly, explain each move and how important it is to take good care of the teeth. Never pry the brush from between the teeth. Wait until the jaws relax, then try again. Our patient sometimes resisted oral care, but if we persisted and were patient, we could finally give a fair cleansing. He would usually spit out the water into the basin, but as his mind became more confused, he would swallow it instead of expelling it. Then we offered him a drink of clear water after the brushing was completed.

2. If the patient has dentures or partial plates, follow this procedure.

a. Provide a denture brush, dentifrice or soap, cool water, waste container, and storage receptacle. Place all of these within easy reach.

b. Bring the patient into an upright position. Unless the patient needs assistance, leave the room and give her some privacy. When the patient has finished with the denture care, remove the equipment, clean it, and put it away.

c. When the patient is unable to care for the dentures, ask her to remove the dentures. If she is unable to do this, the caregiver must gently release the suction of the dentures and remove them.

d. Hold the denture under running water and over a

plastic basin partially filled with water to avoid breakage if you should drop the denture. To soak the denture follow directions on the package of cleaner.

e. Rinse the denture in cold water.

f. Rinse the patient's mouth with warm water or diluted mouthwash.

g. Moisten the denture with cool water and return to the patient's mouth or give it to her to replace. At night, if the patient wants the denture removed, clean the denture and place it in a container, such as a plastic Cool Whip container, and put it in a safe place out of sight.

3. When the patient is no longer able to respond, such as during terminal illness, it is still important to cleanse the mouth.

a. For the patient's natural teeth we used "Toothettes" or a similar disposable device obtainable at the pharmacy, instead of a toothbrush. It is a small sponge on a twisted vinyl handle, similar to that used on a sucker.

b. Glycerine products tend to dry the mouth so we used liquid colace, a mild laxative, which you may purchase at the pharmacy with the doctor's order. It has a pleasant flavor, foams on the toothette and is harmless if swallowed.

c. Place a few drops of the colace in a medicine cup, absorb it with the toothette and sponge the patient's teeth, gums, areas between the teeth and cheeks, and the tongue.

d. Rinse the toothette and squeeze it on a paper towel. Then dip the toothette in clear, warm water and repeat this process until the mouth seems clear of foam.

e. If the patient is still able to drink a small amount of water without strangling, then give a very small amount with a syringe or dropper. If she is unable to swallow, drip a small amount of lukewarm water across the teeth and just inside the lower lip. This will keep the mouth moist.

f. The colace may also be used to swab out the mouth when the dentures have been removed.

g. Always remove dentures immediately if the patient is complaining of nausea or is vomiting.

h. Extreme care must be taken in introducing liquids into the mouth if the patient is in an unresponsive or semicomatose condition. Bring the patient into as upright a position as possible and use a syringe or dropper to give water. Note rate and depth of respiration. Also note the patient's color after the change of position.

i. If the patient does not swallow, even with such assistance as stroking the throat under the chin, consult your physician before proceeding.

Evening Care

1. For the bedfast patient, choose a time suitable to the patient's schedule and to the convenience of the nurse or caregiver.

   a. Remove daytime clothing and turn the patient on her back.

   b. Elevate the head of the bed and proceed as instructed with dental care.

   c. Lower the head of the bed and give the prescribed catheter care if the patient is using a retention catheter.

   d. Wash the face and hands with clear, warm water. Dry.

   e. If the day has been warm and/or the patient's skin is damp from perspiration, sponge the patient all over with clear, warm water, then dry the skin thoroughly. Protect the bed as during the bath.

   f. Apply the external catheter if using this method for the night.

   g. Turn the patient on her side, wash the back, using a warm, wet cloth and lotion. Give a soothing, firm back rub with lotion.

   h. Put on the night clothing or help the patient to do so.

   i. Give medications as prescribed. The patient needs

adequate rest and if, because of the nature of the illness, she needs to relax and sleep, your physician will prescribe a suitable nonhabit-forming medication which will insure a restful sleep. Throughout three years, we used a small dose of a mild tranquilizer. Occasionally it was necessary to increase the amount or to give it during the day during times of agitation and/or stress. When the patient's condition became more normal, we reduced the amount of the medication.

j. Following medications, give the patient a glass of water or juice. Chart the amount.

k. Empty the urinary drainage bag and chart the amount of urine.

l. Turn your patient on the side on which she is to sleep for the first hours of the night. (This instruction is for the patient who does not move herself unaided.) Support the back with the propping pillow as instructed. Slightly flex the knees and place a small pillow between the feet to keep them from touching each other. If the patient might pull on the catheter, place a baby crib pillow over the area, and also be sure the patient's up-arm is supported with a small pillow. Ease the down-arm and shoulder out from under the patient so that it is in a comfortable position. These precautions are for the immobile patient.

m. Adjust the head pillow in a comfortable position, supporting the neck and head without strain.

n. Raise the head of the bed slightly.

o. Leave a night light on. The patient should not be left in complete darkness.

2. The final moments of evening care are important. They may be used according to your faith, the needs of your patient, and your relationship to him or her. Before turning off the lights, I always read aloud to my husband for a few minutes, depending on the interest with which he responded. If he was not responsive, I read enough to be sure that if there were a chance he was hearing me, it would leave him with a comforting feeling. I read simple things, often a

familiar poem, a Psalm, or a story from one of the Gospels. This was a time to offer words of peace and rest, of joy and love. I held his hand and prayed a prayer of blessing. Sometimes he would join me in saying the words of the Lord's Prayer or the 23rd Psalm, even if he remembered just a few of the words. He could often repeat these words when he seemed unable to express himself or comprehend anything else. Sometimes when he seemed the least responsive, he would surprise me by saying, "Amen" or "Thank you," "Praise the Lord" or "I love you!" I would speak lovingly to him, holding his hand, then kiss him "goodnight" and turn down the lights. Two of our daughters, when home together, had made a cassette tape, one of them playing the piano accompaniment, and both singing together so beautifully many of our great old church hymns with which their father was familiar and had sung. Every night for almost two years, when I turned off the lights, I started that tape playing. Sometimes I sat with him and listened or sang along. Sometimes he would say about a favorite hymn, "That's our song!" Other music can be used in this way. I always proceeded on the premise that in the subconscious or unconscious mind the patient hears and is responsive to more than we know. That music was the last thing he heard as he fell asleep.

3. Perhaps this is the place to say something which I will emphasize again. Never discuss a patient's condition or anything concerning her in her hearing or even in her room. The sense of hearing is the last sensory perception the patient loses and she may be frightened or disturbed by comments she does not understand fully. Do not carry on conversations with visitors at the bedside. These "over-the-head" conversations may come through like garbled chatter to the patient who is unable to respond and hears only a babble of voices. It is upsetting. Be honest with the patient's questions about her illness. Do not discuss disturbing news unless the patient is mentally alert and the information will be important and necessary for her to know. Do talk about pleasant, interesting happenings.

4. Be sensitive to the needs of the mobile patient at bed-time.

   a. It is important that the elderly or infirm patient have adequate rest. She may have a well-established routine for going to bed. This person will get ready for bed at the time she feels the need to do so. You will soon know how much help you need to give.

   b. Help the patient with any prescribed medications.

   c. Give any help needed in care of dentures.

   d. If going to bed is not preceded by a bath at which time you have given a good back rub, offer to rub the patient's back. I did this while Grandma sat on the side of her bed. She always seemed to enjoy it. Use lotion. The back rub is refreshing and relaxing.

   e. Remember that for many years of her life, she has tucked children and grandchildren into bed, heard their prayers, told a story or sung a song. Now it is your turn to offer a short bit of reading, say some cheerful and loving words, and give a loving "goodnight" kiss. Make the last words at night cheerful and pleasant.

   f. Leave a night light on for the person who may need to get up at night to go to the bathroom, or have a lamp or light switch within easy reach. For elderly people, the night awakening may be confusing.

Importance of Exercise

A complication of advanced age, physical disability, or weakness related to convalescence from illness or surgery is lack of exercise. The person may become lazy because of the effort required to overcome fatigue and physical problems, or may experience disinterest and unwillingness to exercise.

1. The elderly, ambulatory patient needs encouragement to walk, starting with a short distance, then gradually increasing the length of the walk. Do not let the person overdo. If necessary, walk with him, going a bit farther each day, and stopping frequently to rest. This applies also to any person who is regaining strength after illness or surgery. If the patient is under a doctor's care, the doctor or consulting therapist will give instructions. If weather permits, take the patient outdoors to walk. If not, encourage walking around the house.

2. For the patient who is unable to walk, but who can sit in a chair, there are arm and neck exercises which he may do. All self-help is beneficial.

3. For the immobile bedfast patient, range-of-motion or passive exercise is indispensable. If there is a possibility that the patient may recover even partial use of legs, arms, and some mobility, these exercises performed for him by the caregiver or nurse will insure that the muscle tone is not lost. Encourage participation.

4. If paralysis or immobility is not reversible, passive exercise will prevent painful and deforming contractures of legs, arms, hands and feet. These exercises will soften rigidity in back muscles and keep some flexibility in joints. If one neglects persistent, patient exercising each day, eventually the patient's legs and arms can be moved only with great pain to the patient. The tension caused by

rigidity is painful and exhausting.

5. On order from your physician, your community health agency or the hospital will help you find a physical therapist who will instruct you or your nursing assistant in the proper technique of passive exercise. Range-of-motion exercise is part of the training curriculum in schools of nursing, so your student nurse will have had some instruction and will know where to find more extensive aids in learning these skills. The student will welcome the opportunity to increase his skill working with your patient. During our three years of home patient care, the nurse or aide helped our patient with passive exercises both morning and evening, especially during the evening care.

6. It is important to have as much communication as possible with the patient during exercise. The patient with even a limited capacity to respond will be able to relax a little more and try a little harder if the time is made pleasant and he is encouraged and praised for each bit of achievement.

Problem Areas and How to Deal with Each

Bowels: Constipation and Other Irregularities

Whether the patient is aged, partially disabled or bedfast, it is essential to establish good bowel habits and procedures.

1. Check with your ambulatory patient concerning possible constipation or other bowel problems, such as liquid stools or dark and tarry stools, which may indicate the presence of old blood. Consult the doctor for proper diet and medication to correct constipation or diarrhea.

2. Our patient is an example of the care required in the case of severe brain damage. Peristalsis, the muscular motion which promotes regular bowel action, seemed to be limited. His diet was soft and/or fluid during the first months of illness and contained no roughage. The bowels were activated by the use of sodium biphosphate enema, which is obtainable at the pharmacy under the brand name Fleet, or some similar preparation. The enema is contained in a disposable, soft plastic bottle equipped with a lubricated tip, directions for use, and visual aids. It is convenient to use and must be prescribed by the doctor, who will also give directions as to how often to use it.

3. Warm the enema by placing the unopened container in a bowl of warm water. The warmth will soften the stool and stimulate the action.

4. Protect the bed with a bath towel placed over a Chux and under the patient's hips. If a bedpan is to be used, place it in easy reach. If a commode, have it ready near the bed. Place an old bath towel on the floor under the commode.

5. Lower the head of the bed. Elevate the patient's hips, either by adjusting the foot of the mechanical bed, or by placing a rolled blanket under the mattress of a regular bed. The longer the enema is retained, the more effective

it will be.

6. Proceed with the enema, following directions.

7. *Caution:* Continued use of enemas as a means of moving the bowels will weaken the normal tone of the bowel, making the patient more dependent upon enemas rather than forming a good bowel habit.

8. When our patient commenced eating a regular diet containing more roughage and fruit, the doctor prescribed for him a stool softener (not a laxative). There are several stool softeners available and the right prescription for your patient will be found with trial.

9. In the morning, before or during the bath, the nurse inserted a prescribed rectal suppository, allowing up to 45 minutes for it to dissolve and stimulate the bowel. We observed the amount of time needed and this determined whether the suppository was inserted before or during the bath. In this way the bath could be completed before transferring the patient to the commode.

10. We administered the stool softener every night at bedtime, but found that every other day was sufficient for the use of the suppository and for a good bowel movement. To establish a good bowel program requires some experimenting and patience, but before long you will know exactly what medication to give and when to give it for the best results. The nurse will help. It must not be neglected. In the event that with your treatment there is still not an adequate bowel movement for three consecutive days, consult your doctor.

11. At the proper time, transfer the patient to the commode. It is important that the commode seat be comfortable and that the patient be seated with good body alignment and, if needed, propped with pillows. Baby crib pillows may be used to support hands and arms. Sometimes a pillow is needed under the patient's feet.

12. If the patient tends to sag forward, tie a long, soft cloth around his waist and chair, and DO NOT leave him alone.

13. With the male patient it will be necessary to remove the catch basin from the runners under the chair seat and place it on the floor on a towel under the patient. It is im-

possible to move the basin after the patient is seated, in order to check results, or to do the clean-up, without hurting the genital organs which drop down below the basin rim.

14. If the patient is secure in the chair, leave the room for a while to give him some privacy. If the patient is comfortable he may spend as much as 30 minutes on the commode. Offer a glass of warm tea to the patient. This is also a good time to change the bed linen.

15. If the bowel is still sluggish and there is no action or it is scanty, it may be necessary to check the content of the lower bowel or to stimulate the bowel action with a digital check or stimulation. The nurse will know how to do this and when it is necessary. The caregiver can learn. Provide a package of nonsterile examining gloves or of finger cots to protect the hand and a lubricant like K & Y Jelly. The digital procedure should not be used frequently, only when there is no bowel action after 20 or 30 minutes.

16. When the bowel movement is completed, if the patient is unable to help himself, the nurse or caregiver cleans the anal area, first with bathroom tissue, then with a soft, warm, wet cloth. Be sure that all fecal matter is removed, leaving the area clean. Dry with a soft cloth.

17. Use this clean-up procedure following a spontaneous bowel evacuation in the bed.

   a. When returning the patient to bed following the bowel movement on the commode, it is wise to place a Chux under the buttock on which the patient will be lying. Place the Chux just in front of and under the area of the anus. Do not leave the Chux under the entire hip unless the patient is passing liquid stools.

   b. Occasionally, there may be an additional bowel movement at this time. The Chux will protect the clean sheet and catch the bowel evacuation. If all is well by the time the patient is turned again, remove the Chux.

   c. Prepare for the clean-up if the bowels have moved, by placing a waste container lined with plastic liner on the bed beside the patient's feet. Place an additional Chux and an open container of moist Baby Towelettes on the bed beside the patient. Place a pan of warm water, a washcloth, towel and soap on a stand by the bed.

d. If the patient is lying on his back turn him to the side from which it will be most convenient to work from behind the patient. If the patient is already on the side, stand behind him so that you can work from that side.

e. With several thicknesses of tissue, wipe away all of the fecal matter possible, placing it on a second Chux and lay it aside in a safe place for a few minutes until you can empty it from the Chux into the toilet.

f. Support the patient's up-hip with one hand, pushing him slightly away from you, then fold the Chux under him so that he is resting on a clean spot. Continue to wipe with the tissue until most of the fecal matter is cleaned off.

g. Still holding the patient's up-hip with one hand, push a clean Chux under the down-hip and, pulling out the Towelettes one at a time from the dispenser, finish the clean-up. Remove all of the waste material and drop it in the waste container.

h. Protect the bed with a Chux, wash the anal area and inner thighs with soap and water, rinse and dry. Dust the area with cornstarch and place a clean Chux under the anal area to protect against another possible evacuation. Complete care by placing pillows again between knees and feet. Cover the patient and raise the head of the bed slightly.

i. Clean the equipment and put it away. You may feel dismayed at your first experience, but this method works well. After one experience you will find the clean-up no more difficult than that of taking care of a baby.

j. Consider the cause of the accident. Is it too much stool softener? Poor results while on the commode? Remember, the patient is not responsible. Never express displeasure or aversion. Tell the patient without any additional comment what has happened.

Urinary Problems

1. It is important to maintain a sufficient output of urine. The patient who is able to function independently should be reminded to drink an adequate amount of water, tea, juice, or other liquid each day in order to insure good kidney and bladder function. Ask the patient's physician how much fluid is required for your patient. Unless directed otherwise, a good rule is to give a minimum of 1,500 cc's, and up to 2,500 or 3,000 cc's daily.

2. In caring for the bedfast patient it is important to measure the intake of fluid and the output of urine. Using a container that is marked with ounces and/or cubic centimeters (cc's), determine how much fluid the patient's drinking glass holds. Then always use that glass or one similar in size when offering the patient a drink.

3. When the woman patient uses a bedpan, pour the urine into a container marked in ounces or cc's for measurement.

4. The urinal, or any other container used to catch urine, also should be marked in ounces or cc's for measurement.

5. The contents of the bedside urinary drainage bag attached to a retention or external catheter must also be measured when being emptied. These procedures take little time and become routine, and they are important in assuring you that the urinary system is functioning properly. The intake of fluids and the output of urine should nearly balance during any 24-hour period.

6. The doctor will usually ask for this information if there is any problem. Directions for charting or keeping the record will be given later.

7. The incontinent patient is unable to control the flow of urine, or may be unable to call for help, or may not be able to handle the urinal successfully. It is possible to prop the urinal to an immobile male patient. Wrap it in a soft cloth, and keep it in place with a folded towel. The propped urinal must be check frequently or it may spill over. If the patient is active in the bed and not alert, this prop is not advised.

8. The external catheter is a partial solution for the incontinent male patient. We used the external catheter at night

for several months and propped the urinal during the day. There are several types of external catheters available at the pharmacy. By following the accompanying instructions, and with a little practice, the caregiver and nurse can learn to apply the catheter properly. The catheter is attached by a tube to the bedside drainage bag. This bag should be replaced about every three weeks, when sediment collects inside the drainage tube. This accumulation interferes with the flow of urine into the drainage bag and also may cause a buildup of bacteria in the tube.

a. The external catheter, left in place for more than overnight will cause heating and the retention of moisture, resulting sometimes in red, irritated abrasions and blisters on the penis.

b. When removing the catheter and washing the genital area at the time of the morning bath, examine the penis carefully for any sign of redness or irritation. Then carefully wash, rinse and dry the genital area. During the day, keep the area clean and dry.

c. Any red spots and blisters on the penis may be treated with hydrogen peroxide, applied to the spot with a Q-Tip. When the peroxide stops bubbling or foaming, rinse and dry the area. Red spots or blisters may also be treated with either Betadine liquid or ointment. These treatments should be used only after consulting your physician. After the doctor has recommended a remedy, you can be free to use it as it is needed without calling again, unless the treatment is ineffective.

d. Cleanliness, dryness, exposure to air, and careful attention will prevent problems.

e. When using an external catheter, occasionally shave off the pubic hair around the base of the penis and on the inside of the thighs to prevent the adhesive on the catheter from sticking to the hair and pulling it.

f. If there should occur a complication of urinary tract infection, causing persistent raw sores and blisters on the glans of the penis, it is advisable to use only the fingers, protected by sterile gloves for cleaning the area and for applying medication. Tiny hair-like fibers from Q-Tips or cotton balls may adhere to the area.

9. For the female patient, the best protection is a disposable, adult diaper, like a Pamper, obtainable at the pharmacy. Do not allow the patient to lie in a wet diaper. Make regular checks and change immediately when wet.

   a. Wash, rinse, and dry the buttocks and genitalia before applying a dry diaper. This will keep the skin in good condition. Lying in a wet bed or diaper frequently, or for a long period of time, is one cause of decubiti, or bed sores.

10. The retention catheter

   a. The most effective device for keeping the bed and the incontinent patient dry during a long-term illness is the indwelling or retention catheter. This catheter must be prescribed by the doctor in charge and inserted by a trained and qualified person.

   b. The doctor will give instructions for the care and the irrigating of the catheter and for the care of the genital area. He will also indicate the length of time the catheter may be used and when to replace it. This varies with the patient and with bladder condition.

   c. Both the caregiver and the nurse can learn the techniques used in the care of the catheter. Cleanliness is extremely important in preventing bacteria from the caregiver's hands from following the catheter tube and passing into the urinary tract. For some types of irrigation, it may be necessary to wear sterile gloves. If at any time we inadvertently touched the catheter tube above the connection with the drainage bag, we immediately wiped the tube with a cotton swab saturated with alcohol.

   d. The urinary drainage bag should be fastened on or near the foot of the bed at the rail, usually on the bottom rail of the bed to prevent the down-flow of urine from backing up into the bladder.

Decubiti (Bed Sores or Pressure Sores): Their Prevention and Cure

1. The emaciated patient, the obese patient, and a patient who tends to collect fluid in the tissues, (a condition termed "edema"), are the most susceptible to decubiti, especially if the patient is bedfast for a long period of time. The best treatment is prevention.

2. The decubitis (egg crate) mattress pad has been described in the section dealing with equipment (page 24). This pad is preferable to the circulating air mattress, which is made of plastic, causes excessive sweating, and lacks resilience (springiness).

   a. Do not use a fitted bottom sheet or tuck the bottom sheet tightly over the sides of the bed, as this prevents circulation of air and defeats the purpose of the decubitis pad. However, it is necessary to tuck the draw sheet under the mattress at both ends to prevent its wrinkling and bunching when moving the patient up in the bed. This will still leave the sheet free on either side of the draw sheet to permit air circulation.

   b. It is helpful to have two sets of the mattress pads if you are using a mattress made in three sections or two full-length mattresses. It is possible to wash a section at a time. Directions will be given later.

   c. Do not use a plastic sheet or Chux over the decubitis pad, under the pull sheet or under the patient's body for any length of time. This, too, causes heating and moisture. If the patient is using a retention catheter, it is not necessary to protect the bed except during the bath or when the patient is using the bedpan or receiving treatment which calls for the use of water on the bed. Then use a protective plastic or Chux and remove it as soon as the care is completed. Directions have been given for protection of the bed in the possibility of an uncontrolled bowel movement.

3. Do not leave the patient lying in one position for more than two or three hours. If he is unable to turn from side to back and to the side again unassisted, then the caregiver or the nurse must turn the patient.

a. After the patient has lain on one side for two hours, turn him onto his back for the next two hours, then to the alternate side for the next two hours. Reverse the procedure. Plan the turns so that feeding the patient or other procedures which require positioning on the back may be done at that time. When finished, then turn again to the side. Of course, this timing is approximate.

b. During the night we turned our patient onto his left side at 9 p.m. and positioned him comfortably. The next turn was made at 1 a.m. when he was turned to his right side. Some circumstances may require shorter intervals between the night turns, but this was sufficient for him, except during a few weeks when we were healing decubiti. Then we also used the prone position, on the abdomen.

c. Early in the morning, we turned him to his back until he had eaten breakfast. The bath followed immediately. The bathing procedure and other activity provided enough movement.

4. Following are directions for turning the patient from one side to the other to his back.

a. Explain to the patient that you are going to help him turn to the back or to the other side.

b. Raise the bed to its highest position and lower the head of the bed to the flat position. Remove the pillow.

c. Loosen the pull sheet on the side away from you. If the patient hangs onto the side rail when you are beginning the turn, place a pillow between the raised rail and the patient.

d. Place your feet about eight inches apart with one foot slightly ahead of the other. Lean over the patient, keeping your body in good alignment, and as close to the patient's body as possible.

e. Roll the far side of the pull sheet toward you and up close to the patient's side. Then, using your hips and legs to absorb the weight, grasp the rolled pull sheet with the hand which is behind the patient's shoulder, and with the other hand, grasp the rolled pull sheet behind the patient's hips. With one steady pull, roll the patient over toward you.

    f. If you wish to position the patient on his back, relax your hold when the patient is in this position. If you are making a turn to the opposite side, continue the steady pull until the patient is in the desired position.

    g. If the patient is positioned on the side, flex the patient's knees slightly, again place a soft pillow between the knees and another between the feet. Adjust the position of the down-shoulder and arm so that it is not under the patient. Adjust the head pillow and be sure the patient is in a comfortable position. Elevate the head of the bed slightly.

    h. Be sure the catheter tube is out of the way and not caught under the patient during the turn and that it is in proper position before covering the patient.

5. Good nutrition also is important in preventing decubiti. A well-balanced diet, cleanliness, dryness, and regular turning are the best prevention.

6. If your patient has been confined to bed in a hospital or nursing home, the bed sores may already be present when you assume home care. Sometimes, no matter how much care is given, the skin will grow tender and with little warning will blister or break. Changes in skin chemistry due to the nature of the illness, emaciation, and inadequate food intake (which increases bony prominences) all increase the possibility of decubiti. A patient in this condition must be carefully checked for any sign of redness, tenderness, or any slight break in the skin at pressure points. Our patient developed three of these small breaks within six hours. At that time, we changed from using the plastic circulating air mattress to the egg crate mattress.

    a. Immediately inform the doctor, accurately describing what you see. The doctor or nurse will suggest treatment, but the final results are the product of good and persistent nursing care.

    b. Our nurse and I tapped several sources of information: our doctor and his skilled nurse; an instructor at the school of nursing; and our daughter, a full-time registered nurse whom we consulted often by telephone.

c. Decubitus treatment varies widely. Never give up. These sores can be healed. If observed early, less time is required for healing. The length of time for healing depends upon how advanced the sores are.

d. Placing the patient on sheepskin helps prevent bed sores.

7. Follow these procedures for treating decubitus ulcers.

a. If the skin is not broken, the red, tender areas are healed by a gentle massage with good skin lotion. Lightly pick up pinches of the flesh around the red spot, stimulating the circulation. Do this each time the patient is turned, or when removing pillows from between knees and ankles. Two good lotions for this are Keri Lotion and Vaseline Intensive Care Lotion.

b. If the skin is broken, apply hydrogen peroxide with a Q-Tip or absorbent cotton. As soon as the peroxide stops foaming, rinse the area with clear water. Allow the air to dry, and leave the covers turned back to expose the area. AIR is the most effective agent for healing skin and the genital area.

c. If the open sore persists, paint it with Tincture of Merthiolate, or Betadine solution, applied with a Q-Tip. Air dry and leave uncovered for a while. The breaks we were treating improved but not enough.

d. We then mixed equal parts of merthiolate and Maalox liquid (a medication often taken internally for stomach ulcers) in a medicine cup. We applied this mixture three or four times a day with a Q-Tip, forming a protective coating over the sores. This treatment should be affirmed by a doctor.

e. In addition to these treatments, use light. A 25-watt lightbulb in a goose-neck lamp provides sufficient drying warmth to help heal the sores. Secure the lamp by placing it either on a stand by the bed, or by tying its base securely under the side rail so that it cannot turn over on the patient. Position the patient so that the affected area is exposed to the light. Paint the area with the desired medication and position the light about 24 inches from the area to be treated. Set a timer for 20 minutes. Repeat on each affected area two or three times a day.

f. If the abrasion is on the tail bone, the buttocks must be held apart in order for the light to reach the sore. Using a half-inch to one-inch-wide surgical or paper tape, carefully pull up the fold of flesh that conceals the sore. Fasten one end of the tape to the skin, then pull the tape firmly across the bed and around the raised bedrail. Apply a second strip about two inches from the first, being careful not to place the tape on the sore spot. Then place a short strip of tape across the two ends where the tape adheres to the flesh. This taping will hold the folds of flesh away from the sore so that it may be exposed to the light. Paper tape is easily removed without causing discomfort or damage to the skin.

g. Be persistent. Sometimes improvement is seen within hours, but keep treating the areas until all signs of redness and any open abrasions have healed. At one time it was necessary to turn our patient to a prone position (face down) for decubitus abrasions. Care must be taken to remove the head pillow and use a small, thin pillow. Turn the patient's head so that he lies with one side of the face down, leaving the nose and mouth unrestricted. Then place a pillow of medium thickness under the patient's chest and elevate the head of the bed slightly.

h. In two or three weeks of using all of these methods, the abrasions were healed and new skin was growing over them. Later, when our patient began to eat a regular diet and gained some weight, the flesh on buttocks and hips firmed up, giving more padding to the bony prominences at pressure points.

i. At any evidence of a soft, tender area that failed to yield to regular massage, we again used the 25-watt lamp. During the following two and one-half years, he never developed another sore.

j. Rubbing pressure areas with lotion, exposure to air, keeping the skin dry, proper protection of ankles, knees and elbows with small pillows, and using an egg crate mattress and possibly a sheepskin all combine to prevent decubiti.

k. NEVER use a sun lamp or infrared lamp. There is danger of burning the skin. Your bedfast patient may not be able to express discomfort, he may sleep during the treatment, or even be unable to feel the burning. A 25-watt light, if forgotten for a time, will not do any harm. However, the light treatment should be carefully timed. Do not be careless with it.

8. Follow these procedures for treating advanced decubitus ulcers.

a. If your bedfast patient arrives at your home with advanced, open decubiti (large, open ulcers), your physician will prescribe another medication and will give you instructions for applying it. The 25-watt light treatment will still be helpful if acceptable to the doctor.

b. An ambulatory patient also may have an open sore or ulcer on the leg, resulting from varicosity (varicose veins) or other circulatory problems. Consult the doctor for proper treatment. These ulcers can also be healed. The usual rule is NO wet compresses or soaking. Keep the area dry and protected with a sterile dressing, with prescribed medication. Again, the light treatment is useful.

c. Be sure when your patient is sitting or napping in a chair that his feet and legs are comfortably elevated on a hassock. In older people, poor circulation in feet and legs is aggravated by sitting with the feet down on the floor longer than the time required for sitting at the table to eat a meal.

Lung Congestion

1. When the patient is unable to move about freely, to sit up frequently, or to walk about, fluids tend to build up in the lungs causing difficulty in breathing. This is not

associated with respiratory infection, although a cold may aggravate the condition. Also, a respiratory infection may develop if measures are not taken quickly to relieve the congestion. Our patient experienced lung congestion several times during the first six months of his illness and again in the final months.

2. The symptoms are difficult or labored respiration accompanied by either a harsh cough, or a loose, rattling cough, caused by the accumulation of mucus in the upper respiratory tract, especially in the back of the throat. Because the patient is unable to cough up and expectorate the mucus, it collects in the throat and mouth and can cause strangling if not removed.

   a. Elevate the head of the bed or prop the patient's back and shoulders on pillows.

   b. If the patient is strangling or unsuccessful in coughing out the mucus, turn him on his side, then elevate the head of the bed or prop the patient's head and shoulders with pillows.

   c. If you can see the accumulation of mucus in the patient's throat and mouth when he coughs, reach carefully into the mouth with a wet paper towel and scoop out the mucus. Drop the used towel into a lined waste container and repeat the procedure with a clean, wet paper towel as often as is necessary until the mucus is removed and the patient is breathing more easily.

   d. Explain to the patient that you are helping him to clear his throat, even if the patient is not responsive. Our patient always seemed to understand that we were trying to relieve his distress. Care must be taken lest the patient bite down on the caregiver's hand. Just be watchful and ready to withdraw the hand quickly. If the patient shows much agitation or lack of control, wait a few minutes until this quiets.

   e. The use of a suction device in home care is not recommended. If used often, or without skill, it will cause excessive dryness in the throat and upper respiratory tract.

   f. Use steam in the room if the cough is tight and dry, or

persistent. NEVER use a teakettle or open pan on an electric plate near the patient's bed or even in the room. There is danger of severe burns to the patient or the caregiver from an overturned kettle. A proper steamer is inexpensive and automatic, and is good equipment always to have in the home for the treatment of a bronchial cold or cough.

g. Follow the directions on the steamer and also the doctor's instructions. Use clear water in the steamer, no medication. After becoming familiar with the symptoms and the doctor's instructions, the caregiver can use this procedure as the need arises. Do not use any decongestants.

h. Frequent turning of the patient, getting him up in the wheelchair or to sit on the edge of the bed, and sitting on the commode all help to prevent lung congestions.

Agitation

1. The patient who has suffered brain damage from injury, stroke or illness may become severely agitated. The symptoms are: disorientation; uncontrollable, violent motion; convulsive jerking, shaking; grabbing at the bedrails in fear of falling; kicking or striking out with the fists. There may be evidence of extreme fear, an effort to get out of bed, incoherent speech and loud cries.

a. As quickly as possible, administer the tranquilizer which previously has been prescribed by the doctor for such an emergency. Give only the recommended dose.

b. Avoid the patient's fists, knees, and feet. Speak patiently in a calm and quiet voice, giving reassurance that you are there and will take care of him. The patient is not aware of his surroundings and is not responding normally. He may be going through a terrifying experience. Agitation is often accompanied by hallucinations in which the patient sees and hears threatening sights and sounds. Explain that this is a frightening dream, and that no one is going to hurt him.

    c. An essential protection for the agitated patient is the use of a restraint to keep him safely in bed and protected from injury resulting from hitting against the bedrails. The restraint is a vest, also called a "posey," made of strong, lightweight mesh, that slips on over the head. It can be fastened to the lower bedrails by the long straps attached to the vest. This restraint also may be safely used for the patient who persists in getting out of bed, although unable to walk. The danger of a bad fall is too great to risk. The restraint permits limited movement.

    d. *Always put the side rails of the bed into the "up" position* when patient care is completed or when you are leaving the room.

    e. Always be sure that the bed is in the low position when you leave the room. Never take for granted that the helpless patient cannot make the effort to get out of bed, or roll too close to the edge of the bed and fall out.

Cognitive Impairment

To better cope with the problems involved in caring for a person with a degenerative neural or brain disease one should understand something of the causes and effect on the patient's actions and attitudes.

Cognitive impairment refers to intellectual decline, or the progressive loss of the ability to control one's thought processes and one's actions. This occurs when disease, stroke, or injury damage the brain cells. The impairment may be caused by tiny blood clots which block the path of normal blood flow to any part of the brain, depriving the brain cells of oxygen. The blood vessels may be blocked by sclerosis, calcium deposits in the blood vessels, commonly called "hardening of the arteries." Sometimes a neurologist refers to these vascular incidents as "insults" in the brain.

    1. The condition must not be confused with terms like "crazy" or "psychotic." It is a physical problem and can happen to anyone, no matter how normally the person has always functioned. It is more frequent in elderly people.

The condition varies in degree and in the length of time before the impairment becomes serious. It is a common cause of much distress and eventually leads to loss of control over physical and mental functions.

2. In some diseases, the patient suffers only cognitive impairment at first: memory loss (not the lapse of memory we all experience at times), confusion, disorientation, personality changes, depression, inability to relate to the family and to one's environment. The body may remain strong and mobile for an indefinite period of time.

   a. This places extra stress on the caregiver. The patient is unable to make appropriate responses, to follow instruction, or act responsibly. But he may be able to unlock any door or restraint, attempt to drive a car or may wander off and not be able to find the way home. The patient may also become aggressive and violent.

   b. The experience of two of my friends who are caring for their husbands at home demonstrates the feeling of many spouses. One man has Alzheimer's disease, the other is convalescing slowly following brain surgery. Each wife voiced her frustration when she said, "It may sound selfish to say this, but I can't help wishing that he were in bed like Ronald was. It would be so much easier." I agree. It takes infinitely more patience and physical energy to work with a person who physically is able to move about but who mentally is incompetent.

3. At the other extreme is the spouse or relative who is alert, able to communicate, but is immobile and helpless physically. Each family situation, each caregiver, each patient, and each disease or accident presents a different set of problems and solutions. I can offer some helpful suggestions, but for instruction and training in your particular set of circumstances ask your providing agency to recommend an appropriate book, workshop or an instructor to assist you.

4. The brain damaged person is not responsible for erratic or unreasonable behavior. He or she may resist any interference such as being moved, washed, or having the teeth

brushed. It *is* essential to give medications and prescribed treatment on schedule, or to intervene in a life-threatening situation, but it is not necessary to insist on any routine care that for the moment is upsetting the patient or causing conflict with the caregiver. The patient's comfort and peace of mind, and that of the caregiver, are more important than any noncritical procedure.

a. I found that the frustration I sometimes experienced in caring for my husband usually occurred when I stubbornly persisted in some unnecessary effort to which he was unreasonably opposed. Even if I finally succeeded in overcoming his resistance, it was not worth the upset that the struggle cost both of us. We both benefited if I waited until he relaxed and forgot his objections and hostility, and I mine.

b. When gentle persuasion fails, do not argue with or threaten the patient into submission. If not coerced he may soon relax, forget the negative reaction, and cooperate. An impatient or angry response by the caregiver will be sensed by the most unresponsive patient and will cause the person additional bewilderment and a sense of rejection. Meeting hostility with hostility is nonproductive.

c. If the patient fights the placing of a restraint, the raising of the bedrails, or any other necessary safety measure, you can say, "This is for your protection." Repeat if necessary, then proceed without arguing. Always move slowly and deliberately and use a calm voice. Agitation is aggravated by the caregiver's excited hurrying around, or frustrated, sharp replies.

5. Your patient at any time may become acutely sensitive to ordinary household sounds, like kitchen clatter, the TV, loud voices or incessant chatter. To his hearing these sounds may come through greatly magnified and distorted, causing stress and actual pain to the nervous system. When you see the person so distressed, reduce unnecessary noise to a minimum and soothe your patient with gentleness and understanding. Also check for other causes of adverse reaction which the patient is unable to

express. Excited pacing and banging the furniture may be caused by the need to use the toilet, and not being able to remember where it is. Ask some obvious "first" questions and you may find out what is needed.

6. Memory loss is one of the early indications of cognitive impairment. It may not be severe at first, just enough to cause the person inconvenience and embarrassment, and the caregiver a lot of frustration. The failure to recognize one's spouse or a long-time friend may cause anxiety and even tears for the caregiver. The condition is usually intermittent. In the three years that I cared for Ronald, I was aware that he almost always knew me, but when he asked "Who are you?" or "Where did you come from?" I would pat his hand, kiss him, and reply, "I am Florine, your wife, and I am taking care of you." That would usually satisfy him, although the fuzziness might last a little longer.

   a. Never ask useless questions like, "Don't you remember who I am?" If your patient is having difficulty recognizing familiar faces, explain this to your respite helper or to visitors before they enter the room, asking that they take no notice of the problem, beyond identifying themselves.

   b. Never ask the patient, "Do you know who this is?" or in any way test his recollection. It is better to introduce a visitor by saying, "John Smith (or Martha) has come to see you." This avoids confusing or embarrassing the patient. A simple introduction will often bring an immediate response and an expression of pleasure.

   c. I felt so good about bringing Ronald home. I expected him to be relieved and happy to be there, even though his impairment was severe. I was disappointed when he failed to know that he was home. Throughout the three years, almost every day he would say to me "Let's get out of here" or "I want to go home" and similar expressions. I told him each time that we were at home. "Honey, you are at home. You were in the hospital for a while but now you are home, and I am taking care of you here." I would point out the familiar pictures on the wall and other items that had always been in the room. He would say, "Yes, I know, but I want to go home."

d. Ronald rarely failed to call me by my name; he knew most of our friends who came to see him. He would look across the street and say, "Burt is putting a new roof on his house. Looks like shakes," but still refuse to accept that he was at home. I learned to take the bright spots in the day, as they came.

7. Just recently I heard an explanation of this confusion from a mental health nurse. She said that the person is really trying to say, "This is all wrong. Nothing is the same anymore. I want to go back to the way things used to be when I had work to do and was useful." This makes sense. It was not the physical environment that was unfamiliar but the life environment that had collapsed around him.

a. One day about a month before Ronald died, he was looking at his hands which no longer functioned. He remarked wistfully, "I don't have anything to do." There was a slight pause, then, "I'm not taking care of anything anymore." He was always a doer, a tinkerer, a mender of things in our home and he took care of me! My tears brimmed as I held his wonderful hands and kissed them and consoled him. "I know how hard it must be for you to lie here without anything to do. But you always took care of all of us and of everything around you. All around are the things you did and cared for. Right now your hands can rest, and it is my turn to take care of you." If we become more aware of how the patient feels we can be more sensitive to the irrational outbreaks and the frustration.

b. You may have other problems involving confusion, disorientation, or negative responses. You will find the way to deal with each one with the least stress by thinking of what is the kindest and the most helpful for your patient.

8. Another source of shock and hurt to a spouse may be the patient's dredging up all the bad language he heard or used in his youth and directing it to the caregiver on the

slightest provocation. Remember that the mentally impaired person is not in control and is using any available means to express his frustration. Abusive language should no more be taken personally than would a baby's temper tantrum. Ignore the remarks, speak some soothing, loving words of reassurance, and continue your care as required. Keep your sense of humor.

   a. Occasionally I defended an aide who was recipient of the abusive language. "Ronald! I won't let you talk like that to Laura. She is trying to help you." With a puzzled look he would reply, "I shouldn't have said that, should I?" His use of profane and abusive language commenced suddenly and lasted about three months, then gradually disappeared.

9. Here are some helpful suggestions in working with a person whose brain function is impaired:

   a. Always speak face-to-face with your patient, not from behind him or her. I had a long-standing bad habit of walking away from Ronald, even out of the room, while I was still talking to him. (This had always irritated him when he was well!) As unresponsive as he might be now, it still aggravated him.

   b. Be a good listener, even when a person's words are incoherent and hard to understand. We can learn to stand or sit still and look into a person's eyes and at his lips, and ask simple questions like "Are you saying . . . ?" or, "Is this what you want?"

   c. When you leave the room, tell your patient that you are leaving the room, where you are going, and what you are going to be doing, so that the person does not feel deserted.

   d. I sometimes pushed Ronald's wheelchair into the living room, gave him a glass of tea, or some apple slices, then played the harp for him. I could practice a little that way and enjoy the music. I knew that he had always liked to hear me play the harp, but now the results were unpredictable. One day he would even ask me to play. The next day he yelled for me to stop, that he couldn't stand that noise any longer. It seemed then as if the vibration of the harp strings and the sounding board was disturbing him. There could have been another reason which demonstrates how we need to look for the real meaning behind a person's words. At times he looked stressful and made an effort to lift his bottom up in the chair. The chair was padded, but he was very thin, and I realized he was growing tired of sitting. Sometimes he could say, "My butt's tired," which meant he wanted to go back to bed.

e. Be sensitive to frequently changing moods. Watch for verbal or facial messages of irritation and don't take the hostility or irritability personally. I failed in this at times. When I talked on and on, emphasizing why he had to do something or not do something, he would say, "Shut up! You talk too much!" My response could be quite childish. I would subside into a remote silence and say nothing at all. He was so quick to catch my eye message and would remark in a very reproachful tone. "Why Florine! I thought you were a Christian!" I needed that rebuke and retreated with a keen sense of shame. It is significant how much more sensitive the impaired patient is to our words and looks than we expect. I am sharing these incidents with you to help you understand how mutual are our problems, and that you need not feel guilty. Our humanity doesn't disappear because we are trying to be super caregivers. Neither should we carelessly ignore our irritations.

10. It is never easy to deal with a brain-damaged person, but your patience will grow with practice and determination. It also helps to talk to someone about it.

11. If the time comes when, even with your deepest commitment to home care, you can no longer carry on, do not feel guilty. Some brain impairment causes such a high degree of agitation as the condition deteriorates over a long period of time that violence and physical resistance go beyond the caregiver's ability or safety to handle. You need to know when your ability to cope has reached its limit.

12. As long as the spouse or other relative for whom you are caring shows some degree of responsiveness, use of hands, or ability to speak coherently, there are many ways of helping both of you to enjoy being together. Ask your Agency on Aging to put you in touch with a therapist who will give you suggestions for simple games your patient can play. You may always have to help "cheat" a bit by playing some of it for the patient, but the participation in games, music, painting, coloring, or any number of diversions will relieve boredom and also prevent a complete withdrawal into depressed inertia. It is worth trying.

Sensory Deprivation

1. Symptoms are: listlessness, dullness, depression, occasional hallucinations, abnormal lengths of naps and loss of appetite. This occurs when a person living alone is unable to move about the home freely to do the work and enjoy the customary activities that once were an important part of his life. If there is a lack of mental alertness, the patient tends to become more and more withdrawn. This listlessness overcomes the person who sits alone in his home day after day, or in a nursing home where there is not enough staff to cover all of the needs and visitors may be few.

2. One of the benefits of home care is that it speaks directly to this problem. We all need companionship, music, conversation, sharing, touching, looking out the window, visits from family and friends, and small tasks. The lack of these is probably the most critical cause of the elderly person's retreat into depressed isolation.

3. Even if the patient is confined to the chair or bed most of the day, he will respond and improve as family members stop periodically to visit while performing household tasks. If the caregiver stops frequently to pat a hand or kiss the cheek, give a word of love, or some small service, the sense of loneliness is alleviated. This is as important as keeping the bed dry and the patient bathed. It is the first and most important benefit of home care.

4. The patient may still enjoy a television program or the

stereo. Interest may not last long. If the patient tires, change to another diversion.

5. Children in the home can share their school papers, hand work, and help in several ways to provide a pleasant few minutes for Grandpa or Grandma.

6. If the patient is able to comprehend a little of the news, be sure to share what is going on in the world. Poor eyesight and deafness tend to isolate the person. Speak clearly and loudly. Take time to read a poem, the family letters, familiar verse and stories from the Bible and tell the neighborhood news. The more mentally alert person responds to and enjoys reading, music, and cheerful, friendly conversation.

7. It is possible to provide every physical care, heal the decubiti, provide good nutrition, and forget the essential ingredients—caring and kindly love.

8. Even an argument or being upset with an obstreperous, stubborn patient is acceptable, as long as it is compensated for by plenty of friendly attention. This makes the situation normal, just like home has always been.

9. The mobile patient who may be unable to live alone and needs help but not total care will enjoy a ride, some friends coming in for tea, a trip to the store, and a chance to go to church, even if the entrance must be made in a wheelchair. Most churches provide a wheelchair for handicapped persons. During the summer when my husband was responsive to being outdoors, the nurse and I placed his wheelchair on the driveway by the house and ate lunch with him from TV trays. He seemed to enjoy that, and it was a change for us. To facilitate moving the wheelchair outside, we installed a ramp from the back door to the driveway to avoid the steps. It was covered with a ribbed rubber runner.

Nutrition and Fluids

A Well-Balanced Diet

The patient's nutrition will depend on three considerations:

1. The diet prescribed by the doctor for any specific problem, such as high blood pressure, low blood pressure, diabetes, obesity or some other condition. Observe the doctor's prescribed diet carefully.

2. The patient's needs, other than those mentioned above: Avoid foods that are fatty, fried, highly seasoned. Avoid an excessive amount of sweets or rich desserts. Provide a well-balanced diet that promotes good bowel function and normal flow of urine. Give patient drinks such as juice, tea and Kool-Aid. Offer fluids between meals, always keeping a record of the intake.

3. The patient's enjoyment of meals: Nutrition must not only supply the body needs, but be tasty, adequate, well-balanced, and pleasant to eat. The sick or elderly person may be a slow eater and food quickly cools. The home offers an advantage here. The food may be the same as that prepared for the rest of the family, or it may omit some item and include another in keeping with the patient's needs. It is served warm and kept palatably warm during mealtime. A Salton or other electric warming tray placed beside the bed or chair keeps the food warm if it is served in a heat-resistant plate.

4. We used a stainless steel divided relish tray as a plate. Care must be taken to disconnect the warmer if the food grows too warm.

   a. If you hand-feed the patient, never place a spoonful of too-warm food in her mouth. Check the temperature of the food frequently.

    b. Homemade cornstarch pudding or tapioca pudding is nutritious and more appealing to the sick person than pastry or rich desserts. Ice cream with simple fruit topping is also good. Plain cookies are easy to eat and take the place of cake, although we always shared a simple birthday cake with our patient. We celebrated his birthday each year with a special dinner served at bedside. Provide plenty of fresh fruit.

    c. Suggestions for dietary requirements may be obtained from the doctor or from a health care center. If the patient is eating a regular diet, cook the same food for her that you do for the rest of the family with the exception of highly seasoned or extra rich foods. Keep in mind your patient's favorite foods, too. Do not overfeed.

5. During the years after my husband retired, he would come in from working in the yard, or arrange to be home from doing errands in time for tea at 3 p.m. This was a very special time for us. When he became ill, I tried to keep this schedule, even when he seemed unresponsive to his surroundings. I took our tea tray to the bedside and said, "It's time for tea!" Often, he would reply as he always had, "Sure, I'll have a cup of tea with you." Sometimes it was a glass of tea served with a straw, and sometimes it had to be poured out a little at a time into a medicine cup for easier delivery. I believe he was aware of these familiar, happy times together.

Feeding the Patient

1. For the bedfast patient who can feed herself, provide an over-bed table and an attractively arranged tray with utensils which the patient can handle easily. Some of the food may be cut into bite-sized portions before serving. Provide napkins and protect clothing and bed with an adequate coverup.

2. If there is a vision problem, tell the patient what food you are serving. See that all she needs is within reach. It may not be necessary for you to remain in the room, but check back occasionally to be sure the patient is managing.

3. If the patient is able to come to the table, even in a wheelchair, there is special pleasure in eating with the family. Never comment on spilled food or in any way embarrass your family member.

Feeding the Helpless Patient

1. Make the tray attractive. Use dishes and table service that are easy to handle. A teaspoon may be preferable to a fork. Offer the food just as the patient would usually eat, a bite of this, a bite of something else, a drink of tea or a sip of juice or milk. Use a napkin when there are drips.

2. If the patient does not see well, or is not mentally alert, always name the food you are offering in the spoon. "This is a bite of oatmeal," or "This is potatoes and gravy," or "Here is a nice bite of chicken."

3. Use deliberate, quiet motions. Remove the spoon from the patient's mouth after each bite very slowly. Do not hurry the eating process. It *is* slow and one wants to get it over with, but with patience one can learn to control the feelings of boredom. This is an important time for a person who has so little to anticipate. It is a good time to show love and cheerfulness. But don't overdo the conversation.

4. There may be times when the mentally incompetent patient will reject food for no apparent reason. Do not argue or scold her. Take the tray back to the kitchen, then return with it in five minutes. By then your patient will probably have forgotten the unwillingness to eat and will consume the entire meal. If not, give the fluids which are essential and wait until the next meal.

5. Adequate nutrition may sometimes require frequent small meals, instead of the customary three meals per day. Be prepared to improvise times and schedules. Give a small meal at the regular time, then nourishing snacks between meals. Slices of pared apple, or sections of orange, or other fruits should be offered between meals.

6. Occasionally a patient may show irritation by clenching the spoon between her teeth. Never try to pry the mouth open to force out the spoon. Let go of the spoon, sit quietly and wait until the jaws relax. Talk to the person patiently,

then gently wiggle the spoon out of the bite. This does not always signal the end of the meal. Often the rest of the food will be eaten without incident. But if the patient spits food out it is better to remove it and wait until the next mealtime.

7. Summary:

Keep food warm.

Feed slowly.

Be cheerful and kind.

Always explain what you are doing and what food is being offered.

Use a napkin frequently to wipe patient's mouth and chin.

Record Keeping (Charting)

Simple but Important

It is important to keep an accurate record of your bedfast patient's condition and of your nursing procedures, especially during any time when the condition is unstable or there are complications. It is not necessary to keep as extensive a chart as that kept in the hospital.

1. A stenographer's notebook is adequate for charting.
2. Place the date at the top of the page. We started charting for a 24-hour period at 1 a.m. when turning the patient for the first time in the night.
3. In the left-hand column, write the amount of fluid intake and the time it was given, including fluids given with meals and those given with medications or between meals and at bedtime.
4. In the right-hand column, write down the amount of urine output and note the time at which the urinal, bedpan, or bedside drainage bag was emptied.
5. On the lower left side of the page record all medications given, including the amount and time they are given.
6. On the lower right side of the page, make any additional notes as required. If it is necessary to take the patient's temperature, pulse, respiration or blood pressure, record each, and the time it was taken. These vital signs usually need to be taken only when problems occur, or if requested by the doctor.
7. Also, note anything unusual: failure to eat, constipation, too frequent bowel movements, or any other problem.

Consultation with Doctor

An accurate record is valuable when consulting the doctor or reviewing the patient's progress.

1. Before calling the doctor, read the chart yourself, then have it at hand by the telephone. Write down what you want to tell the doctor. If it is a critical change, give him the most acute symptoms first. Report any life-threatening problem: heart problem, severe pain, breathing difficulty, hemorrhage, sudden loss of consciousness, seizures, or a sudden elevation or drop in blood pressure.
2. Briefly review the past three days, reporting intake and output and other symptoms, such as change in temperature, pulse and respiration rates, in addition to blood pressure, if this has been taken. Report any bowel problem that is an unusual occurrence in your patient. Be brief; the doctor does not need a wordy description. Answer his questions concisely without offering your opinion.
3. Write down his instructions.

Monitoring Blood Pressure

1. To take the patient's blood pressure, you will need a blood pressure cuff with a barometer, and a stethoscope. Ordinarily you would not have these items in the home. Your student nurse may own them and be glad to bring them to the home when he comes to work, if the doctor requests that the blood pressure be taken regularly. The first-year student nurse receives instruction in the use of a stethoscope and in taking blood pressure readings.
2. If this help is not available, the doctor will request that a qualified person from the health agency visit the home. This person will bring his own equipment. The doctor will advise you if he wants a regular blood pressure check.
3. Proper techniques for taking temperature, pulse, and respiration should be demonstrated person-to-person for the benefit of the caregiver in the home. The student nurse or the qualified instructor from the home nursing department of the local health agency can give this instruction.
4. If the patient has a chronic blood pressure problem, requiring daily checks, there should be a blood pressure kit in the home and the home caregiver should learn this technique.

Medications

Medications should always be administered and taken with care. Following are some guidelines to remind you of basic precautions and procedures.

1. Keep medications out of reach of children, mentally incompetent or cognitively impaired patients whose memory may be faulty, or those who may have poor eyesight.
2. *Never* give any home remedy or medicine that was not ordered for your patient by the attending physician, even if it is something that made Aunt Mary feel better.
3. Following are the *Five "Rights" of Administering Medication* (instructions given to nurses):
   a. Right medication
   b. Right time
   c. Right patient (at home that may be no problem unless you have two!)
   d. Right dose
   e. Right route of administration (by mouth, or injection, etc.)
4. Follow instructions correctly. Give medications at the times and frequency prescribed by the doctor.
   a. Measure accurately.
   b. Keep a careful record of the medication you give your patient.
   c. If you notice any adverse side effects, discontinue the medication immediately and notify the doctor.
   d. You are responsible to give the required amount of liquid needed with the medication, or to see that the mobile patient is taking the required amount. Some medications upset the stomach if taken without sufficient water, milk, juice, or food.

e. Before using the last of any medication, ask the doctor if she wants the prescription renewed. If so, purchase the refill so that the patient does not miss a dose.

f. If your immobile patient is unable to swallow pills or capsules, remind your doctor of this when she prescribes the medication. Most medications may be obtained in a liquid form. If not, crush the pill between two spoons, or empty the capsule, and give in a spoonful of applesauce or pudding. Give fluids as usual.

Important Safety Measures

Safety in the Bedroom

1. Always raise the side rails of the hospital bed to their "up" position, and LOWER the bed to its lowest position when leaving the room or completing patient care. It is never safe to assume that the patient cannot fall out of bed or make an effort to get out of bed.
2. When the helpless or incompetent patient is sitting in a chair, wheelchair or on the commode, make certain that he cannot fall forward. In some instances, this may mean tying the patient into the chair with a long, soft cloth.

Safety in the Bathroom

1. Never leave a weak or infirm person alone in the bathtub or shower.
2. Use safety bars or handgrips in tub or shower for the elderly, mobile patient, or provide secure assistance.
3. Be sure that bath mats and rugs cannot slip and that the bathtub is made skidproof.
4. Always test water temperature before patient gets into tub or shower.

General Safety Measures

1. If there are children in the home, make sure that all toys are kept in their place. Keep the areas where the elderly person walks from room to room and to the bathroom or table free from obstacles over which a person with poor eyesight or coordination can stumble.
2. Keep stairways clear and see that no objects are lying on the stairs or on the floor in front of the stairs. Footstools, chairs, and small tables, left near a place of transit, can cause painful bumps and falls.

3. Keep medications out of reach. Never place a thermometer in the mouth of a patient who is not completely alert and competent. Take a rectal or axillary (armpit) temperature reading and adjust it. Subtract one degree from registered rectal temperature; add one degree to registered axillary temperature reading. Allow five minutes to register temperature reading.

4. If the patient is able to walk and take some responsibility but is forgetful, or becomes confused, he may open doors and wander away, leave the area and become lost. To prevent this, keep the doors locked, screen securely fastened, and the yard gate (if there is one) barred. This is a simple precaution and will save time spent in looking for a lost family member, as well as safeguard the person from injury in a serious fall, or from a passing car.

Conclusion

This small book contains a large part of my experience as a wife, caring for my husband at home for three years. It is also my experience in caring for his aged mother during a part of that time, when she was no longer able to live alone.

I have written in everyday language for families who want their loved ones to live out their days in happiness and dignity, surrounded by familiar things, and with love and warmth.

I have shared from my own experience the learning of skills, the finding of resources for help, and the satisfaction I received in bringing comfort and help to my husband in his time of greatest need.

I have omitted some details which would be important to the care of your patient who has problems which I have not encountered. Your family doctor, or a staff member of the local home health agency, will provide you with information and instruction applicable to your patient's unique needs.

I undertook the responsibility for my husband's home care just three months before my 70th birthday; weight, 115 pounds; health, good. I completed my nursing service three months before my 73rd birthday. Age is not a problem if one has reasonably good health.

I have personally used every piece of equipment and every procedure which I have described. with the following exceptions:

1. Transferring the patient from bed to chair or commode and back to bed without the use of a mechanical lift. My size and muscle power was not sufficient to make this a safe procedure for the patient or for me. However, I usually was present to assist the person doing the transferring.
2. Inserting a retention catheter, a procedure reserved for a physician or a qualified nurse.

3. Monitoring blood pressure. I had no need for this skill, but the technique can be learned by the caregiver if necessary.

You will master the basic skills as you do what is required of you each day, and you will find that you are more capable in nursing care than you ever imagined you could be.

Never attempt to do anything for which you do not have the physical strength or the necessary knowledge or skill. There may be some areas of care other than ones already mentioned (such as giving medication by hypodermic injection) which will require the help of a qualified nurse. Common sense plays an important part in your success. Use it, and do not hesitate to ask a skilled person for instruction and/or help. In an emergency, keep cool and do the best you can until help arrives.

Live one day at a time. It is essential for inner peace and assurance that you take each day's events and duties as they come. Good will, faith, and a cheerful acceptance of each day will help free you from stress and from discontent with your present situation.

There is a good kind of physical weariness that corrects itself with a short nap, a few hours of sound sleep at night, a brisk walk, or a change of scenery.

Fatigue and depression are usually an affliction of the spirit and come from anxiety, stress, inner rejection of life as it is, fretting over the change in lifestyle, or resentment and irritation toward someone or ones who seem to be leaving it all to you. For the person or persons whom you feel should be more help, try openness and honest communication regarding the problem, rather than angry reproaches, or feeling sorry for yourself, or indulging in a bit of martyrdom. All such inner and outer conflicts are resolved with persistent applications of good will and thankfulness that you are able to give such an important service to those you love.

It was difficult for me to sit quietly, wearing sterile gloves which prevented me from doing anything else, and wait just ten minutes for the completion of a catheter irrigation. I learned to look at the pictures of our children and grandchildren which filled the wall above Ronald's bed. I sent my love to each one, silently giving thanks for their love and asking God's blessing on each young life. Music from the stereo was restful, too, and eased the boredom.

At times when I was tired but sat at the bedside for forty-five minutes feeding Ronald, I found it restful to talk to him about our love and the good times we had shared during the years, rather than fretting over the lengthy feeding process.

I did not always keep a calm spirit. Sometimes my patience was stretched to the limit as yours will be. Sometimes I was impatient with him, even though I knew that he was not responsible for his negative responses. Afterwards I felt guilty, even though I had apologized in tears. During the first year, Ronald's student nurse pointed out to me several times that I was a human being, dealing with a brain-damaged person, and that it was all right that I occasionally gave way to impatience, anxiety and weariness. I had to learn to accept my negative reactions, too.

I did not always have it all put together, but I knew the resources for finding inner strength and love enough to carry on with good feelings. These resources never fail us if we put our trust in them.

I assumed this responsibility because to me the alternative of a nursing home for Ronald was unthinkable. His hard work and care had provided this home for us and for our children. He belonged here as long as I could assure him the necessary care.

For every hour or day of difficulty, there have been many more of deep satisfaction in having kept my commitment and in the knowledge that my husband received the finest care possible during the last three years of his life.

I believe that I grew in love and maturity, not in spite of but because of the challenge of each day. Now that it is all over, the three years seem short, and as I look back I see in them one of the most rewarding and enriching experiences of my life.

Friends dropped in to visit or help, and as we sat over afternoon tea together, our friendships deepened into a relationship we had not known before. Another dividend was the lasting friendship formed with our part-time housekeeper and her young family. Joyce was quick and efficient, and she always looked for ways to help and to relieve me for a rest period. She became amazingly sensitive to Ronald's needs and helped in his care as if he were her own.

Another continuing benefit is that of a Lenten study group which I was asked by our church to host for six weeks. It was an opportunity for me to be involved while I was confined to home. We had all known each other for many years, but we grew in warmth and love and communication so that, instead of the weekly meeting ending after Lent, we have continued meeting for four years. These 14 friends who gather in our home each week have been an unfailing source of support and cheer. It has been a mutual experience in a community of love that we would not have known had it not been for one of life's difficulties.

Our family, although living at a distance from us and from each other, seemed drawn closer together during the illness of their father and grandfather, as we all shared our concern, our love, and our family purpose. The frequent phone calls and periodic visits from our children and from my brother and sister-in-law were a welcome support. Sometimes Ronald could listen and respond to the phone calls, and until the last few days of his life he was aware and responsive to the love and comfort he received from each visit.

The resulting closure was expressed later by one of our daughters in a letter: "There is something to be said for nature's crises, for they remind us of important things. I do know that with the onset of Daddy's illness, I realized a new sense of family, a new perspective which gave most unpleasantries a context not enjoyed before, and illuminated the positive things. Although much of that comes with time and age, it is always good to have a fuller picture of what one has taken from the early home out into the world.

"Perhaps even more important was the chance you gave me to give back what I am capable of giving. I did gain a realization, too, of that which I am not capable of giving, all good lessons. I think that to be able to repay 'in kind' (in the manner of support and present care) is not always possible for children, and we all know of cases in which it is just not allowed by parents. So I am very glad that you asked me to come that July, that you let me do what I could, and that you stuck to your guns in the face of our arguments.'' (She refers to the initial reluctance to let me undertake the home care.)

Because national economic restrictions may result in cutbacks in the funds which subsidize the care of the sick and elderly, home care becomes a humane and attractive alternative to the nursing home. With the growing understanding of the emotional and physical needs of the ill and elderly, there is growing support for the benefits of family care as preferable to that of any institution.

Before the need arises, the family needs to discuss feelings and evaluate the depth of compasssion and willingness to make such a commitment. Often there are indications of approaching physical or mental decline, which give us time to plan and make decisions. This is also a time to enroll in a home nursing course. Sometimes, as in our case, the unexpected happens and we have to make a quick decision. But long before this emergency arose, my husband and I had been committed to home care for each other.

On the basis of this kind of caring, many family units will stretch their boundaries to include those family members who have made their contribution to the nurture, the growth and the education of the family through the years. They now deserve some golden days, even though their physical and mental powers are slowing down and no longer are serving them well enough to warrant their living alone. They still have something of great value to give us, in creating for their children and grandchildren the opportunity for unselfish service, and in our homes a new horizon of family devotion and commitment.

Appendix A

Resources for Obtaining Assistance in Home Care

Because public health agencies vary from state to state and in different cities, I will list only general resources to explore for finding the services you may need. The directors of the agencies which I contacted were helpful in making suggestions or in directing me to other sources. They will help you as well.

Schools, Hospitals, Agencies

In *Securing Adequate Help in the Home,* I suggested the local college School of Nursing as a possible source of nursing help. Also, the hospital's registry of aides and nurses who are looking for part-time employment. Professional agencies, e.g., Kelly, Upjohn, Quality Care, etc., are listed under NURSES in the yellow pages.

Home Health Agency

In virtually every area there is a Regional, District or County Home Health Agency, which is affiliated with the national agency.

1. The Home Health Agency provides comprehensive in-home services to homebound residents under its jurisdiction and to those who are caring for the home patient.
2. Any patient of any age and living within the district, who would benefit from professional and supportive home care on an intermittent basis, is eligible for these services.
3. Patients are usually referred to the agency by hospital or physician, but families who are assuming home care may contact the agency and be advised of proper procedures of obtaining its services.
4. All cases referred to the agency receive an initial assess-

ment visit by a Registered Nurse. If skilled services are needed, a plan of treatment is established with the physician in charge.

5. A priority of the Home Health Agency is the instruction of the home caregiver and the family. This is of value if the home care has been assumed in an emergency without opportunity for preparation. A skilled visiting nurse makes regular visits to observe the medical condition if this is needed, and to carry out treatments and procedures which require a qualified nurse. The nurse will give instructions in nutrition, special diets, diabetic care, skin care, exercise regimens, and comfort measures. This is valuable help in the areas for which I have recommended one-to-one demonstration of procedures and techniques, such as patient transfer and the monitoring of vital signs (temperature, respiration, pulse and blood pressure.)

6. Other services include occupational therapy and speech therapy. Some agencies have a Medical Social Worker who can provide further assistance with community resources and financial needs.

7. A certified Home Health Agency may be part of the local health department, connected with the local hospital, or it may be an independent entity.

8. COSTS: Both Parts A and B Medicare cover the costs of the full range of home services according to existing guidelines.

    a. Medicaid is still available for those of limited or no income who are not eligible for Medicare. This help is given according to specified guidelines.

    b. Private insurance covers costs specified in the policy.

    c. If the patient is not eligible for any of these, sometimes the area United Way can help.

    d. State departments of Social and Health Services differ from state to state. Sometimes they provide Medicaid, food stamps, and "chore service," such as housecleaning and some minimal "hands-on" care.

Other Resources

1. The department of Social and Health Services may be able

to direct you to a service which will provide sick-room equipment without charge if the family is unable to pay for it, including hospital bed, wheelchair, commode, oxygen tank, even a patient lift. This also needs a doctor's orders.

2. The American Cancer Society provides some help for cancer patients and will counsel and assist the home caregiver.

3. In many communities there is a hospice-type service for support in the home care of terminally ill patients. This is a developing movement, and may be located by calling the Social Services Department of the hospital.

4. United Way and the Veteran's Administration are also possible souces of assistance for patients ineligible for any other financial aid.

5. In every community there are Senior Citizen groups or programs. They may be located by consulting the telephone directory or one of the public agencies. They offer a variety of services which will be of help to the home caregiver and the patient.

6. The local chapter of the American Red Cross in many communities offers free or low cost, short-term courses in home nursing. The classes comprise about sixteen hours of intensive instruction and are available on demand to any group of seven to sixteen persons, including teenagers as well as men and women. This training is valuable in caring for the young family as well as in the eventual care of the aged or disabled at home.

Aid to the Visually Handicapped

1. If your patient is legally blind, visually handicapped, or physically handicapped (unable to hold a book for any length of time or to turn pages, or has a severe reading disability), call the public library nearest you and ask for assistance. The librarian will give you the address and telephone number of the State Regional Library for the Blind and Physically Handicapped.

2. Eligibility must be certified by a doctor of medicine.

3. A wide variety of services is provided: Large print books, talking books, radio reading service and other helps.

Brochure and application forms are sent on request.
4. The State Commission for the Blind works with people in the home to help them function more independently.

Agency on Aging

This provides a national network for further information on local and state senior services. The Agency also helps to develop programs and short-term workshops for the benefit of caregivers who need instruction in specific kinds of care. In some cities or counties the Agency on Aging contracts with providing agencies for needed services which have been properly documented, and helps with the funding. The Agency directors encourage caregivers to let them know about their problems and they actively seek out caregivers so that they may make them aware of this important service and of helpful workshops. When undertaking home care, inform this agency.

1. A family member's critical illness or collapse of mental ability may immediately impose on a spouse or other relatives responsibilities for which they are unprepared. In addition to decisions regarding ongoing care of the patient, one is also confronted with a changeover in finance management, the obtaining of legal authorization, as in power-of-attorney, and the frustration experienced in filling out unfamiliar forms, as in Medicare. A call to the Agency on Aging will provide helpful information and sources to contact for assistance.

2. Another important resource for helping the family or the individual who is caring for a patient suffering from a long-term, degenerative disease is that of a support group. Such groups create a caring and understanding climate in which the caregiver, the family, and often the patient, can come together to share their problems, their feelings, and inspiration. This is a growing movement. Some of these groups are:

   a. ASIST (Alzheimer Support Information Service Team) designed to help individuals and families of persons suffering from Alzheimer's disease.

   b. Wil-Cope helps to meet the needs of persons who have Parkinson's disease, and helps their families to understand the unique needs of the patient.

   c. Hospice, which I have already mentioned, is a growing group movement directed by highly qualified staff people. It endeavors to meet the emotional and physical needs of cancer patients and their families. Hospice seeks creative ways in which to live during treatment, remission, and the final stages of the disease, including an honest and compassionate confrontation with death and dying. The movement is of immeasurable help to both patient and family.

3. Families and individuals caring for persons with multiple sclerosis are also forming support groups in many communities. Patients and families can meet together to give each other emotional support and encouragement, and to develop creative programs and share information.

4. Patients who are incapacitated to any degree from a stroke are encouraged to join a support group. These groups which include the patient, caregiver, and the family are beneficial in relieving depression, promoting rehabilitation and in encouraging the patient.

5. For those families who are caring for someone with any other neural disorder or crippling disease there may be no specific support group available, but any of the above would welcome you to be a part of their fellowship. Much of the content of the group's discussions and sharing will apply to any basic longterm illness. If you do not know of anyone to whom you can talk, ask the director of the Agency on Aging to help you find someone. You may even form a group with some other families whom you know to be facing similar concerns. It is such a help to people to find out that they are not alone, and that someone else with a similar life-changing situation cares enough to reach out to others.

6. I have listed some of the resources for obtaining assistance. Explore your community agencies and organizations, using the telephone directory or any information about which you read or hear. If you live in a rural community contact the Agency on Aging, and the Home Health Agency in your county and ask for their assistance.

Appendix B

The Needs of the Caregiver

Caregivers with whom I talk are usually weary and often discouraged from the lack of emotional support and the difficulty of finding dependable help in caring for their patient. The mountain of responsibility seems so great, their best efforts ineffective, and their need of respite unmet. Some say that they almost never leave the house for relaxation. The caregiver is most often a spouse caring for husband or wife after the family is grown and living at a distance, or an adult child caring for one or both elderly parents.

Many caregivers are unaware of available resources for assistance. Some agency directors have told me, "We could do more if the caregivers just called us." It is for this purpose I have made a general list of possible resources you may find wherever you live. If you are in a more isolated rural area, call your health agency in the county seat. If provided services in any community are inadequate, the caregiver's insistence of need may stimulate greater effort to recruit volunteers and to expand the bank of qualified, part-time, employable aides.

1. If the patient is bedfast the caregiver needs competent part-time nursing assistance, the amount and kind determined by the caregiver's needs and the patient's condition. She may also need some chore service and additional respite help. The caregiver for the infirm elderly person needing minimal care may also need chore service and a respite helper.

2. The family involved in caring for an elderly relative in the home needs occasional time together for relaxation apart from their patient. The change renews and refreshes them in the long-term commitment.

3. A critical illness or accident usually brings immediate response from family, friends, and community, in offers to

help, gifts of food, frequent visits and phone calls. Then, as the crisis tapers off into long-term care the help sometimes dwindles as people turn to new critical needs, leaving the caregiver with less support. It is important then for the caregiver to plug into the providing agencies, and to request renewed volunteer help through church or service-oriented social groups.

4. The caregiver needs positive emotional support. Well-meaning friends often say, "You shouldn't try to do this. You will break down under the strain," or, "I just ache for you—you are carrying such a terrible burden," or, "You know you have your own life to live, too." Even medical and nursing staff may discourage the caregiver. When one caregiver appealed to the family doctor for a more effective tranquilizer for her patient, his response was, "You know, I told you not to try to take care of him at home." A visiting nurse repeatedly asked another caregiver, "When are you going to give up?" Such negative attitudes can so undermine the confidence of the caregiver, making her doubt her ability to continue, that she can scarcely face getting out of bed in the morning. The caregiver deserves positive, cheerful reassurance from family, friends, and professional providers, including the minister of her church, and the offer of help either by professionals, or from respite volunteers. Words of admiration and appreciation for her determined effort will do more to lift her spirits then all of the well-meant sympathy.

5. Relief from grief, anger, sagging spirits, and feelings of futility is experienced when the caregiver learns to live one day at a time, and to accept the present situation as a meaningful part of life. Terminal illness can be a time of preparation for eventual separation, a time for bonding, and for healing the wounds we cause each other in the unavoidable conflicts of relationship. We receive new insights in the proximity of death, and in the hands-on service we give to a loved one. The inner spirit is revived when we accept with good will our role as caregiver, and discover new depths of love, of compassion, and of growth in patience and unselfishness.

6. Sometimes a patient's family living in the same area fails to offer help or to respond to the caregiver's request for assistance. The caregiver may want to consider the underlying cause of this reluctance and perhaps take the initiative in helping to develop a new relationship. A lively, growing sense of relationship and outreach in the family is one of the rewards of home care.

7. Many caregivers have feelings of anger and guilt for a variety of reasons. Guilt is most often felt when the caregiver is forced to relinquish the home care of a family member to that of an institution. Guilt feelings are destructive and must be resolved. When you know that you have done all you can and that you are willing to heal the past and flow with the future, deal honestly with your feelings and trust that there is a good purpose at work beyond your sight. Talk about your feelings with an understanding and compassionate friend or counselor who will help you resolve your inner distress.

8. I have mentioned in my own story the inner resources I tapped in times of weariness or discouragement. For your own enrichment and for sharing with your patient, use a book of brief, positive affirmations of trust and love; a book of inspiring poetry; the Bible, whose pages yield countless assurances of provision for every need. You will discover as I did, that your inner appeal for strength, for insight in solving problems, and for enough love to carry on will bring release from anxiety and the assurance that you are not alone.

Important Telephone Numbers

Keep by the telephone a list of telephone numbers frequently called, or for emergency:

Doctor
Nurse or Aide
Ambulance
Family Members
Minister, Priest, or Rabbi
Volunteers—and any others you consult

Appendix C

Cost Comparisons

I made a limited survey of costs for patient care in six of the best nursing homes in our community. These figures will vary in different states and in different cities, and they may be inflated by the time you read this, but they offer an idea of the financial outlay.

Nursing Home

Charges for a full bed-care patient are from $40 to $58 per day, or approximately $1,200 to $1,740 per month. This includes room, board, and nursing care.

1. Additional charges are made for personal sickroom supplies, such as catheters, bedside urinary drainage bags, lotions, etc. and all medications. Some nursing homes provide laundry, hair care, and feeding the patient; others make an additional charge. There is usually an additional charge for regular physical therapy.

Home Care

In the care of a full bed-care patient in our home, I have included the salaries of the nurses, a part-time housekeeper, the Social Security tax, State and Federal Unemployment Tax paid on each employee and the cost of all the large equipment. Then I deducted the reimbursements from Medicare or from selling the equipment when we no longer needed it. The final total was approximately $953 per month. I did not include the cost of food in our case because that remained about the same as before the illness. However, there can be additional food costs if at any time meals are supplied for personnel. I did not keep an account of this.

Ambulatory Patient

For the ambulatory patient who requires minimal assistance, the cost differences are greater.

1. Light care in the nursing homes which I surveyed costs from $35 to $37 per day, or about $1,085 to $1,150 per month, with additional charges for supplies, some personal services and medications.

2. In home care, the expense would be only for food and an occasional helper to relieve the primary caregiver. If the patient was already residing in the home the food costs would remain the same. Some additional equipment might be needed. This would vary.

3. A portion of the patient's Social Security benefits would cover any such costs and also that for medication and equipment.

4. In home care, if the patient needs total bed care and the cost of part-time nursing and other help is more than the patient's benefits and family income will cover, application could be made to the State Social Services for additional help and this agency would advise the patient or caregiver. At present, subsistence is limited to "chore service."

Appendix D

Instructions for Washing the Decubitus Mattress

If the mattress is one made in three sections, any section which becomes soiled or wet may be washed by hand by one person. If the mattress is made in one full length, it may be washed, but it would be easier to handle if two people worked together.

Fill the bathtub about one-third full with warm water. Add any mild dish washing detergent, such as Ivory, Joy or something similar, to make a light suds. Place one section at a time in the solution. Push the section up and down in the water, squeezing and submerging. Let the water out of the tub, pushing the section back and forth to press out as much water as possible. Then run clear water in the tub for rinsing. Allow the water to drain out again, pushing the mattress against the side of the tub to squeeze out all the water possible. Repeat until it is almost entirely rinsed.

At this point, I folded the pad and placed it in a plastic tub to prevent its dripping on the floor and carried it to the automatic washer. It could easily be fitted into our machine. I filled the washer with water on the rinse cycle, placed it on "gentle spin" and let it run through the rinse cycle. This did not damage the mattress as much as putting it through the entire wash cycle. When the spin was finished, I laid the mattress across a lawn chair outdoors in the sunshine and turned it occasionally until it dried. It was not difficult to wash three sections in rotation this way. Note: a full-length mattress pad will not fit in the washer.

The mattress did not need to be washed frequently, because of the protection we gave it, but accidents did happen. We found it necessary in a long-term use to have two complete mattresses, as it does take several hours to dry, depending on the atmospere and the amount of sun. Sometimes we had to put it outside on the second day to complete the drying process.

Part Two

An Adventure in Love

There was little warning of the impending crisis in our lives—a few weeks of unaccustomed fatigue, some weight loss, nothing alarming. Two incidents of oppressive chest tightness had forced Ronald off the riding mower and into the house. But the doctor's examination revealed no problem. His blood pressure and the EKG were as normal as usual. Our doctor told him to stay off the mower.

Six months earlier, on January 2, 1977, we had celebrated our 50th wedding anniversary with a joyous, rollicking reunion of our entire family from Christmas Eve through New Year's Day. Ronald and I were healthy, active, involved in church and community. We travelled to visit our children, and sometimes to far places. We anticipated many more years of this satisfying life.

Now I sat beside him in the hospital, experiencing numbing shock, disbelief, and a sense of unreality. My healthy, active husband was stricken with a brain-damaging illness which our doctor, a neurologist, and an internist had not been able to diagnose in spite of innumerable tests. The C.A.T. scans revealed extensive brain damage but not a cause.

His speech was unintelligible, his responses confused. He had lapsed into a semiconscious condition with spiking temperature, labored respiration, and severe apnea. He appeared to be dying. Our family doctor, Robert Sullivan, concerned and perplexed, watched with me and we agreed that in the event of a life-threatening crisis we would take no extraordinary measures to prolong his life.

At home that night I walked the floor in wrenching anguish as I thought of the imminent separation. At the same time I was reaching out to the Resource of all Love and Strength, and I experienced a deep awareness that nothing could happen to us outside of God's love and care. Then peace came.

In the morning I called Miriam as she had asked me to do if I needed her. She was the only one of our four daughters who worked independently during the summer. Late in the afternoon she arrived at the hospital in an aura of love and support that lifted my sagging spirits. Her father, too, was aware of her presence and held her close.

We tried to celebrate his 75th birthday on the following day but he did not respond. We had called Miriam's sisters, Nyle, Janette, and Ann to report his condition. They all came home, bringing an indescribable warmth of love and comfort.

There was no panic, just an outpouring of their love and concern as they gathered around their dad's bed. Remarkably, Ronald's speech became normal and he was sitting up in bed when they went in to see him. They began to sing to him—we had always sung when we were together. They sang the beautiful, familiar hymns that he loved, and he sang with them. The sounds of the singing drifted down the hospital corridors and nurses stopped to listen.

That crisis, the first of many, passed. At home we sat around the table, talking about life with Ronald and without him, and found that we could all laugh and cry at the same time.

During the next few days they sat with their dad, talked to the doctors, read the results of the tests and the C.A.T. scans. Then, one by one, three went back to their responsibilities at home while Miriam stayed on with me. A few days later her 16-year-old daughter, Lisa, also came to help.

Ronald's stay in the hospital, with no confirmed diagnosis or positive treatment, was drawing to a close. Dr. Sullivan recommended that I send Ronald to an extended care facility. I had planned to care for him at home, but there was a chorus of protest from the doctor and from our girls. "You can't do it. It will be too much for you. You would need a strong man on each of three shifts just to lift him!"

At this time Ronald was showing some improvement again. We decided to move him to a health care center which offered a program of transfer therapy. If the therapy were successful, I would be able to move him from bed to chair or commode, perhaps even to the bathroom in a walker, making it possible for me to care for him at home.

It was wishful thinking and the results were negative. By the time the ambulance arrived at the nursing home with him, he had again lapsed into unconsciousness. Each day he vacillated from deep sleep to severe agitation and spiking temperature. I dared not leave him alone except for a few hours at night. He was unable to press the signal button or to call out for a nurse. The facility was just not equipped to provide total care for a helpless patient. I was the one to give it.

How could I sit there, wait on him day after day, with no place to lie down for a rest or to put my feet up? My thoughts became scattered and turbulent, and I had to hold tightly to my trust in order to pull myself together.

Janette, who was a registered nurse employed in a hospital, had come home again. She and Miriam had been looking after Granny at home and coming in each day to give me some relief. This day when they arrived I had made my decision. I exclaimed, "This will drive me up the wall! I will not leave him here. I want to take him home where he belongs and try to restore some order to our lives."

There was no protest. They and our doctor all agreed that no matter how great the task might be at home, the resources of strength in our home environment would offset the physical stress I might experience in such an undertaking.

About 15 months prior to the onset of Ronald's illness, his 97-year-old mother's near blindness and the disabilities of old age made it unsafe for her to live any longer alone in her own home. Her dread of going to a nursing home and the difficulty of finding a live-in companion whom she would accept, outweighed her reluctance to leave her home and live with us. Later, even with Ronald's illness, I continued to care for her until her death in our home a few days before her 100th birthday.

When she came to live with us we had placed a bed for her in our den. We now moved her bed to the dining room and converted the den into a room for Ronald. Jan shopped for needed supplies. I rented an electric hospital bed, called an ambulance, and brought him home to begin our great adventure. I have never regretted my decision and I count those three years as a rewarding time of growth, of learning, and of satisfaction in fulfilling an important commitment.

Our first need was for a part-time nursing assistant. I called Clark Community College School of Nursing, and although the school was in summer recess, they were able to help me contact Harvey Varner, a licensed electrician who had decided on a career change. Harvey had finished his first year of nurse's training, and was looking for a part-time job. The day after we brought Ronald home, Harvey walked into our home, glowing with confidence and concern. He has never walked out of our family.

Harvey was right for the job and the job was right for him, increasing his nursing experience during his formal training. His response to family and patient was spontaneously warm and we reciprocated. We planned our care program around his class and clinical schedule. Before he left us, after his graduation, he trained a prenursing student, Coralee, to take his place; then later he trained Roy, another prenursing student.

In 1942, I had enrolled in a Red Cross home nursing class where I learned the basic skills that prepared me to care for my mother in our home during the five months of her terminal illness in 1944. One never forgets such training. I contributed all that I had acquired in home nursing and Harvey shared with us the skills and enthusiasm he received in his daily instruction. We conferred, we shared; we tapped several sources for professional direction as needed: my daughter, Jan, by phone; our doctor and his nurse, and our urologist; Harvey's instructor in the school of nursing, and the visiting nurse from our Home Health Agency, who later came once a week while Ronald was under the care of the physical therapist.

It was a team effort. Together we overcame difficulties, learned by trial through failure and success, innovated techniques for coping with problems. Every day brought a new challenge, not to survive, but to succeed.

I still have a dozen stenographic notebooks, kept by my assistants and me, which hold the record of more than a thousand days and nights of home care. They are simple charts but surrounding them is the aura of loving and effective response to my husband's needs.

If this sounds too well organized and simple, I can say that home care, of either a long-term, helpless bed patient, or of a mobile, self-help elderly person, is never easy. One doesn't look for ease but for reasonable solutions to every problem, and the ultimate satisfaction of having brought comfort and help to a loved family member.

I learned to live one day at a time. It was essential to accept our new life cheerfully, to daily commit in faith the anxiety I often felt, the grief that I experienced in seeing my husband of more than 50 years incompetent, disoriented, and helpless.

I proceeded on the premise that when my patient seemed unaware of his surroundings or even of my presence, deep inside he knew that he was in my care and surrounded by love. Often I received a glimmer of assurance that he knew.

Our goal was to keep his body comfortable, and to feed his spirit in every possible way. I could not endure the thought of his awakening at night in a strange place with no familiar face and voice to comfort him. When I turned him in the night, I would sometimes find him awake and I would ask him if he wanted me to sit with him for a while. He would reply, "Would you, please?"

I found my comfort in his warm handclasp. I fed him pudding while I drank hot chocolate. I would sing a favorite song or repeat a cherished Bible verse. I could tell him how much I loved him, and hear his familiar reply, "I love you too." This was one of the rewards, just to share his companionship.

I had times of frustration and irritation with Ronald when he was obstreperous and hostile. Then my hands were not too gentle as I settled him down, and I could hear my voice becoming shrill. I immediately felt grieved and would put my arms around him, kiss him, and tell him how sorry I was that I had been cross with him. I knew that he understood, but the tears came with guilty feelings, especially when he would say, "I didn't act very nice, I'm sorry."

Once when he was agitated and fighting everything I did as I cared for him, he kicked me hard in the chin with his knee.

In a flash I whacked his bare bottom with my hand. I felt awful about that and told him so, even though it did put an end temporarily to his fractiousness. It taught me two things: to keep my face out of the way and that I had to be more aware of his frustrations and despair as well as my own frustration. These times of failure on my part were fleeting compared with the hours of satisfaction I experienced in caring for him. I wish I could blot them out. I can only accept them.

We had plenty of problems. The care varied according to the needs. We faced every kind of complication during the first six months other than heart ailment, high blood pressure, or other organic disease, and the complications intensified during the last six months.

In every crisis I could rely on Harvey's competent help, on long-distance conferences with Jan, on the unfailing help of Dr. Sullivan and our urologist, Dr. Fitzgerald, and on the help of the Home Health visiting nurse.

I accepted gladly the offers of help from friends. No one can assume this responsibilty alone. Two of my friends came every Friday for three years to sit with Ronald while I had my hair done and ran errands. When I came home they had tea ready and we visited and shared the week's happenings. Often we could include Ronald in our tea time in his room.

My neighbor from across the street came every evening at 9 for two years to help me position Ronald for the night because it usually involved a full body lift to bring him up in bed. During the last year when we had a live-in nurse, he came on the nurse's day off. It made the last duties of the night so much easier. Since then I have been able to give these good neighbors some help in times of need. None of us can live to ourselves and find real joy in life.

Our children and grandchildren contributed much to us, with their visits, phone calls, letters, cassette tapes, and warm love and concern. In every family there are hurts, unintentional wounding in time of emotional stress, misunderstandings often buried in the past, sibling or parent-child conflict, which need healing. Our family experienced much closure and a new bonding in our time of trouble. This kind of love withstands any strain.

There were wonderful assurances from God's word on which I leaned hard. No matter how difficult the day or how tired I was I could fill my mind with peace as I recalled the ancient words, "As thy day is, so shall thy strength be," or as I repeated the words of a Psalm which popped into my mind when I needed it most.

In a little while I would be aware of a new surge of strength and calm assurance. There deepened in my consciousness an assurance that this life is not all and that we were both being prepared for the ultimate death that is part of life.

About six months after the onset of his illness, Ronald's condition improved in several areas. First, he reached for his glass of juice and I found that he was able to convey it to his mouth and drink without spilling. Then his chewing and swallowing functions returned, and on a regular diet he gained weight.

One morning he was suddenly alert and asked, "Where am I? What has happened to me? How come I'm such a cripple?" He listened attentively as I explained about his illness, and then he asked, "How long have I been in bed?" He cried a little when I told him how many months had gone by, then expressed concern for me and for the work it had made for me. He wanted to know if I had enough money to take care of everything.

I reassured him that everything was in good shape and how thankful I was and how important it was to me that I could care for him. Of course, he forgot all of this in a little while and he kept asking the same questions, but I was happy to answer again. We had some communication.

Although Ronald's memory of conversations or events from hour to hour seemed to be a total loss, he often recalled events from his youth, or spoke about his business and associates, the church, and family. Sometimes he quoted a Psalm, or a favorite Bible verse.

Throughout his illness he frequently relived his past painful experiences. One time I found him sobbing, tears streaming down his flushed cheeks. I wiped his face with a cool cloth and held his hand while he explained, "Dad sold my horse!" I re-

minded him that the loss of his horse and her foal had happened 60 years ago, and we talked about it until he was com-
forted. Sometimes he relived his father's death in 1938. His
sorrow was as vivid to him as if it were today. How thankful I
am that in such a time of distress I was there to help him.

There were other occasions when the recall was happy.
Harvey would encourage him to talk about his youth on the
farm, the hard work, the fun, the Halloween pranks. The sharing brightened his day.

For about six months he responded well to my reading to
him. I began cautiously, not knowing if he really understood. I
read my diaries of our travels and found that he liked to go
back over our experiences. Then I read favorite poetry, short
stories, an adventure article from the *National Geographic,* the
Bible, and eventually full-length books. He liked James Her-
riot and Paul Gallico. He was quick to let me know if something didn't interest him, which was an indication of how well
he was listening. Often he remembered what we had read the
day before, and sometimes even asked me to read to him.

Then one day he said, "I hope you are getting more out of
this than I am." I laid the book down and asked him, "You
aren't able to follow it, are you?" "No." That ended this wonderful time of reading together. I was a little sad but so thankful for six months of more consistent awareness, for it had
shown in other areas, too.

I continued to read to him, especially in the evening before
he was ready to fall asleep. Short poems, stories from the
Gospels, familiar passages from the Psalms and other Old
Testament poetry. Often he would repeat the Lord's Prayer
when I started it, or the 23rd Psalm. Even toward the end of
his life he was making an effort to say the words and he remembered much of these.

When we prayed together before I turned off the lights at
night, he would sometimes make his own prayer, and it was
usually comprehensive and understandable. He might quietly
comment, "I don't understand what has happened to me, but
praise the Lord, anyway!"

When I played the cassette tape which Nyle and Miriam
had made for him, or one with the family singing at our an-

niversary celebration, he would unexpectedly say, "That's our song!"

On Christmas morning we seated him in his wheelchair in front of the fire and the Christmas tree while the few of us there opened gifts and sang together. He did not always seem aware, but it was important that he be included and I felt sure that the familiar family Christmas reached him in some measure. Each year on his birthday I made a cake and had something special on his tray. Sometimes he knew, sometimes not. We observed our moments for tea at three o'clock every afternoon. Ronald was usually pleased to have me sit by him and drink tea with him. Even when he could no longer drink it from his glass I gave it to him with a plunger-type syringe.

On warm days when we went outside with the wheelchair, Ronald would often comment on the flowers he knew so well, about the trees, and on what was going on in the neighbor's yard, showing that he did know that he was at home. Almost every day he told me that he wanted to go home, yet he was quick to see something in a room or across the street that he recognized. All of this confirmed for me the benefits of caring for him in his own home surrounded by the familiar. And especially the importance to me of being with him at all hours of the day or night when he would become aware of my presence, of his own needs, and sometimes of his fears.

I wanted to talk about the reality of death and what it would mean, but he spoke of it only in the first weeks of his illness, and then to Miriam. He said, "I know I am going to die. I just don't want to be alone." Miriam held him in her arms and assured him, "Daddy, we will never leave you alone. We will be right here with you when the time comes."

During the exceptional six months of increased cognizance and activity, Ronald spent four weeks in the Rehabilitation Institute of Oregon (RIO), an affiliate of Good Samaritan Hospital in Portland. He seemed so much better, and under the guidance of a physical therapist we had been getting him up in a walker. With much help he finally could walk to the table for the evening meal. His mother was pleased because she could sit there with him.

He was accepted at RIO for intensive therapy. After the

preliminary examination and review of case history, the medical director told me that they could see no way that he would ever walk alone again or even be able to sit up alone. Ronald worked hard in therapy and progressed so far as manuevering his wheelchair down the hall alone. I went in for training in doing a sliding board transfer, and we went home with high hopes. Again my hopes were unfulfilled. When we came home I could not transfer him from his bed with its egg crate mattress to anything. In the hospital the transfer was from a hard bench, which made a difference.

But we did have one great adventure. Our grandson in Honolulu was to graduate from high school and Nyle and Roy begged me to bring Ronald. They just wanted him to have one more visit with them where he had enjoyed so many happy days. I'm not sure today how I had the sheer guts to start out, but I did. So that he wouldn't tire too quickly I gave him 25mg of thorazine when we left home and another 25 halfway there. He knew where we were going and did very well on the plane. All transferring was by aisle or stair chair. He was fitted with a leg bag and external catheter.

The arrival at the airport was touching. Our daughter, Nyle, and our little great-grandson put leis around his neck and Ronald's tears trickled down his cheeks.

I had plenty of help bathing him, getting him in his chair and to the table. We ordered a Handicab to take us to the yacht harbor where we could wheel him up and down the walks so that he could see the boats, the sea, and the surfers. Then he said that he was tired and we went home. Of course, he couldn't attend graduation, but on our last Sunday evening we had a front table for Emma's beautiful show in which Nyle played the harp at the Royal Hawaiian Hotel. Emma, a close friend of Nyle's, had seen us before the show, put her arms around Ronald, kissed him and called him "Dad." She and Nyle had worked together for a long time and we had often thrilled at her glorious voice. This time she sang two lovely songs with only harp accompaniment, which she dedicated to "Mom and Dad." Ronald was quiet throughout and had no expression other than dullness. But when Emma came to sit at our table afterwards, he suddenly leaned toward her and said,

"Emma, I think you sang better tonight than I have ever heard you!" None of us could restrain the tears. It was worth the whole enormous effort, and it was the last one.

When we went home the vacillation again occurred. Ronald lost his ability to feed himself and showed deterioration in other ways. During the next years there were times of responsiveness, but never like those of that six months.

His mother was still able to do many things for herself, but I knew that the anxiety she suffered with the traumatic illness of her son, her only child, was taking its toll. Her mind was alert and I watched over her carefully. She still enjoyed visiting a dear friend each weekend but was finding it more difficult to walk because of some lack of balance. First, she depended on her cane; then, after a stormy struggle with her, I insisted that she use the walker. I needed to do more to companion her but there was so little time. I did maintain the evening care, the back rubs at bedtime, and attempts to share all I could with her regarding our family, the letters and phone calls. I occasionally invited her friends to call. She never understood why we couldn't make Ronald well, and I felt deeply that she believed we were neglecting him, even though she knew that his care was my top priority.

Then just three days before Christmas in 1978, Grandma had a stroke. Even then her mental power decreased quite gradually over a period of hours. She could let me know when she needed to use the toilet but could not walk to the bathroom, and each time that I helped her to the commode which I had placed by her bed, I had to lift more. The next morning Dr. Sullivan said, "Enough!" and admitted her to the hospital. Miriam came home that day for Christmas, and she and I took turns going to the hospital to check on her. She never regained any meaningful consciousness again, but I continued telling her that I would take care of her as long as she lived.

The day came when she no longer could remain in the hospital. I kept my promise to her that I would never let her go to a nursing home. I ordered another electric hospital bed, placed it in the dining room in place of her little studio couch and began the treatment of the bed sores she had acquired in the hospital. The day she came home we had a severe ice storm.

My current aide and Joyce, my part-time housekeeper who was always my unfailing helper, especially with Grandma, could not get a car out of the garage or get to a bus. And I was alone with my two patients.

For some reason it seemed like an adventure, and I decided I would do what I could and not worry about what I couldn't do. Grandma could not eat or drink more than a teaspoon of tea at a time, so that eliminated the long feeding process. But at that time I knew I needed more help and I called the Home Health Agency. In spite of the ice, the visiting nurse arrived within 30 minutes, bringing me a big dose of encouragement. She changed Grandma's indwelling catheter and gave me a promise of help with the baths. The ice melted that night, and the aide and Joyce both returned. A week later, just a few days before her 100th birthday, Ronald's mother died quietly with her head resting in my hands. I had kept my promise to her and found it deeply satisfying.

During the last six months of Ronald's life there were times when I wondered as I sat beside him, "How long can this go on?" And sometimes he would say, "How long is it going to be?" "When will this end?"

It was important that I be aware of his incredible weariness and boredom in spite of every effort we made to provide some diversion and relief.

Occasionally, I could talk to him about the day coming when he would know release from his weariness and helplessness. I longed for this for him, as well as for my own release from the strength-consuming daily provision for his comfort. I knew how sorely I would miss him, but I also was honest in acknowledging, without guilt feelings, that both of us would welcome release. When I occasionally felt depressed about our circumstances I called up a great assurance from one of the Psalms, "My times are in Thy hands," and I rested in the knowledge that even this period in our lives was not without purpose and meaning.

Although our daughters and grandchildren had come quite regularly to see us, at this time Anni felt a strong urge to come home again, a complicated trip for her. Her dad was overjoyed to see her, although prior to her coming he had not seemed to notice anyone or recognize even me, some of the time. She spent every minute in his room, feeding him, snuggling against him, singing to him. It was rewarding to her that she could talk to him and find him responding even though he was so very weak.

Jan came the next week and spent time with him. It was obvious to her that his periods of awareness were few. Soon after she left, Nyle came from Honolulu and once more Ronald rallied his forces to show his pleasure at her being there.

While Nyle was home there came the severe test of my commitment not to use extraordinary measures to prolong life in a medical crisis. About ten days before his death, Ronald was sleeping much of the time and for several days had taken only liquids because of his difficulty in swallowing. He didn't open his eyes when I carefully fed him. I continued verbally expressing my love, reminding him that each of his daughters had been home to see him. I am sure that his inner hearing picked up the sound of my voice and the reassurance that we were all near. Occasionally, even then, he spoke, saying "Thank you" for something we had done for him.

Late one evening, the slight bleeding we had noticed occasionally coming from the bladder through the catheter increased to a profuse flow. I called our urologist immediately and he said to bring him to the hospital emergency room. Nyle went with me as we followed the ambulance to the hospital.

Dr. Fitzgerald passed a new catheter and I stood across the table while he irrigated the bladder with normal saline to stop the bleeding and prevent clotting. After an hour and a half the bleeding was not diminished and I sensed the doctor's concern as he announced, "I have only one alternative—take him to surgery, anesthetize him and see if I can find the artery and cauterize it."

Without hesitation I said, "No." He looked surprised and asked, "Why?" I explained that we had all confirmed that with Ronald's condition as it was and in view of his long, weary, deteriorating struggle, we would not take heroic measures to keep him alive.

The doctor asked me, "How would your children feel about this?" and I told him that this was a mutual commitment.

Then he said, "You've made the right decision." Later he told Jan that he did not think her father would have survived the surgery. How thankful I am that he did not have to die in surgery.

He gave me detailed instruction for continuing the irrigations every 20 minutes around the clock. In a few minutes we were home again. Roy, our live-in student nurse, was up waiting for us and he and I took turns through the night with the treatment that would prevent severe pain from clotting.

I called Jan at 5 that morning, and in a few hours she came to take over for the day while Roy and I slept a little. By late afternoon the bleeding stopped and Ronald's blood pressure began to rise. Miriam also came for two days, then once more I was alone.

A week later there was a recurrence. This time I started the irrigations myself and reported to the doctor. Through the night we kept the saline flowing in and out of the catheter. Ronald was sleeping and comfortable. It was then that I felt the impact of my decision. It was as if I were watching his life ebb away through that tube and could do nothing to prevent it. I knew I was doing the right thing, and that there was no alternative, but I cannot minimize the grave sense of responsibility I felt, and the universal empathy with every person who chooses to disconnect a life-support system. Eventually the bleeding stopped but it had left Ronald profoundly weak.

For the next days I gave him what nourishment he could safely swallow, then even that ended. I often talked to him about his coming adventure as he walked out of this life into a wonderful new joy. I will always remember the morning I bent over him, holding his face gently between my hands and kissed him, saying, "Honey, I do love you so very much." What joy I felt when his lips slowly moved and with great difficulty he formed the words which he was unable to say aloud, "I—love—you."

It was a warm, golden, August evening, when all alone with him, I was turning him on his side. I knew that the time had come. I held his hand, kissed him and once more told him that I loved him. At that moment he died with a gentle outgoing of breath. It was a time of fulfillment for both of us, and I will always be grateful for the privilege of caring for him, my adventure in love.

This was our Daddy, our Grandpa, and our Great-Grandpa. But most of all, he was Mama's husband for 53 years, and for the last three years their lives were bonded together in a drama of love, devotion, and hope. Daddy now knows the fullness of all joys, and for him, Mama, we thank you. May your heart be light and may your eyes laugh at sorrow.

—The concluding words of the family's tribute to Ronald, written and spoken by Miriam at the memorial service.